Great
with
Money

Great with Money

6 Steps to Lifetime Success & Prosperity

ELLEN ROGIN, CPA/CFP®

AND MELISSA BURKE, ESQ/CFP®

Two Tango
PRODUCTIONS

Published by Two Tango Productions, Northfield, IL

Prosperity Circle is a registered trademark.

Cover Design: Kirsten Ford, Focus Design
Layout Design: Sharon Page

Photo Credits
Ellen Rogin: Linda Schwartz Photography
Melissa Burke: Namascar Shaktini

Library of Congress Control Number: 2012940914

ISBN-13: 978-0-9815181-3-8

Printed in the United States of America

10 9 8 7 6 5 4 3 2

Dedication

Ellen

To Steven, Benjy, and Amy—
I am so blessed to have you as my family

Melissa

To Lulu
and all who hold the light

Important Disclosures

The information contained in this book should not be construed as personalized investment advice, and should not be considered as a solicitation to buy or sell any security or engage in a particular investment strategy.

The opinions expressed in this book are those of the authors only and there is no guarantee that the views and opinions expressed in this book will succeed.

No investment or financial planning strategy can assure success or protect against loss in declining markets. The strategies and concepts articulated in this book are for educational and illustrative purposes only and are not intended to provide financial, legal, or tax advice. Individuals are encouraged to seek professional guidance concerning their own unique situation.

The stories shared within this book are based on real situations. However, the names have been changed to protect the individual's identity and the facts may have been altered to better demonstrate the particular message being conveyed.

Contents

The Prosperity Circle®

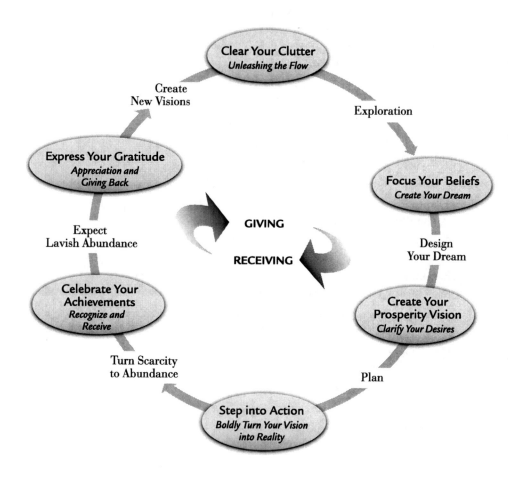

Create
New Visions

Clear Your Clutter
Unleashing the Flow

Exploration

Express Your Gratitude
*Appreciation and
Giving Back*

Focus Your Beliefs
Create Your Dream

GIVING

Expect
Lavish Abundance

RECEIVING

Design
Your Dream

Celebrate Your
Achievements
*Recognize and
Receive*

Create Your
Prosperity Vision
Clarify Your Desires

Turn Scarcity
to Abundance

Plan

Step into Action
*Boldly Turn Your Vision
into Reality*

Introduction

Would you like to be *Great with Money*? Most people we know say that they would love to be great with money but what does that really mean? Is it just about having massive amounts of wealth? We don't believe so. Is it being a sophisticated investor, current on all the latest economic trends? No, it's not that either.

After many years of practical experience, we have grown to understand that being truly great with money means having a prosperous mind-set and confident approach to money rather than an amount of money in the bank or specific investments in a portfolio.

We have learned too that many people have an uneasy and often complicated relationship with their money. People tend to experience great anxiety as well as great joy when it comes to their financial lives.

Through our work, as well as through leading workshops for hundreds of people over the years, we have observed how common it is for people to experience a sense of lack or scarcity and have great angst around money. Sometimes they articulated this to us and sometimes the angst is evidenced by their actions (or inaction). Often people fear not having enough to provide for themselves as they grow older. Others lack knowledge and hesitate to make decisions. Some are missing an organized plan or are paralyzed by concern of losing whatever they have accumulated. These fears make it challenging for people to make sound financial decisions, often affect their relationships, and can cause sleepless nights.

Most surprisingly, we noticed that these feelings of lack and fear are experienced by very wealthy people as well as by those of lesser financial means. If anyone believes that money will solve all of their issues, we are sorry to break the news, but they could actually have millions and millions of dollars and still worry about not having enough.

On the other hand, there are people who consistently set and meet their goals and feel great contentment regardless of their actual net worth. These people tend to be extremely grateful for what they have in their lives and focus attention on what is working well rather than on fears of what might happen. They live with a sense of ongoing abundance and joy. This has inspired us to share our fundamental belief that money worries or contentment spring most of all from a money mind-set. A prosperous outlook accompanied with financial knowledge and tools *will* help to move individuals forward confidently and abundantly.

The realization that money can work in beautiful ways for people—in support of dreams for them, their families, and their community—led us to explore ways to have a more lasting impact on people's abilities to maintain this crucial mind-set of prosperity. Again, this type of financial abundance is measured not simply in dollars but in contentment as well.

We examined the industry further and questioned whether the right kind of help to design lifetime abundance was being provided. We found that the typical, left-brain financial planning approach takes a look at goals and objectives (typically ones that people are *supposed* to have, such as retirement and funding the kids' education). Yet this approach ignores the question of what might hold someone back from creating their dream. Nor does it help in honest envisioning and articulation of what someone may want to accomplish in the first place. Instead, the most common approaches to financial planning jump right into running financial projections, implementing investment strategies, and choosing products.

Our own professional training—Ellen's in economics, accounting, and as a CERTIFIED FINANCIAL PLANNER™ professional and Melissa's in business law, estate planning, and consulting—was grounded in traditional analytical problem solving. We both quickly realized that, in order to do our best work, we needed to broaden our viewpoints about money and about how to better assist people to plan in more meaningful ways. To make an analogy to holistic medicine, we realize that an East-meets-West approach to finances can support people in ways that the more conventional methods are simply unable to do.

While traditional financial planning is valuable and the support a good advisor can provide is important, to be great with money requires more. It requires individuals to play the role of designer of their life, to manage their money mind-set and more, and to be confident in the ability to lead a prosperous life. **The information in this book offers a new viewpoint on money, meant to be far greater and more meaningful than merely managing money successfully.**

Many people have either lost, or never learned that they have the power within themselves to be the source for abundance in their lives. We all possess the innate capability to create and keep the flow of prosperity working to support our dreams. After identifying these missing gaps in information on how to be truly great with money, based on real-life experiences, we developed a creative strategy that can be used any time, at any point in life. And not just in financial affairs. This book offers a lifetime process to help with financial creation and contentment. We call it the Prosperity Circle®. By following the steps along the Prosperity Circle, people will have the tools to create, build, and sustain abundance in their lives. Each step is clearly outlined, along with specific strategies to help build the life each person dreams of and to have their money work to help provide support along the way.

The Prosperity Circle strategy teaches the fundamental steps, chapter by chapter, that are necessary to become great with money:

- Everyone needs to *Clear out the Clutter*—both physical and mental—in their life.
- Everyone's *Beliefs and Focus* of attention on money issues require honest exploration—at least to bring them into consciousness to better direct their prosperity journey.
- Everyone needs to grow their *Vision* from the *inside* most of all. Only then can they create an honest *Action Plan* that will detail the successful steps needed to move their dream into reality.
- A *Vision* without *Action Steps* is merely a wish. Action minus a dream leads to living someone else's vision.
- And everyone will need to understand how to recognize and *Celebrate Achievements* when the results manifest.
- Then add further to abundance by circulating *Gratitude and Appreciation* to others through lifetime acts of *Giving and Receiving* along with practicing your own brand of philanthropy.

Over the years people have reported great successes to us from using this strategy and tools. We have incorporated many of their stories in this book. In order to maintain the confidentiality of these individuals, we have changed their names as well as some characteristics of their stories.

By sharing these ideas, we hope that everyone will use these tools to create lavish abundance in their life and to have money become a force for good in the world. Enjoy playing with these concepts and shift from anxiety to joy in every aspect of life!

CHAPTER 1

The Secret to Limitless Prosperity
Giving and Receiving

Clear Your Clutter
Unleashing the Flow

Focus Your Beliefs
Create Your Dream

Express Your Gratitude
Appreciation and Giving Back

GIVING

RECEIVING

Celebrate Your Achievements
Recognize and Receive

Create Your Prosperity Vision
Clarify Your Desires

Step into Action
Boldly Turn Your Vision into Reality

THERE IS ONE THING we want everyone to know right from the start: being great with money is actually quite simple. Most people believe it requires some innate skill or many years of study and experience. This is a money myth. People who are great with money simply think and act in specific and intentional ways—ways this book will show—that those who are *not* great with money fail to do. By following the steps of the Prosperity Circle you will learn what people who are great with money already know. You can totally transform your life by earnestly walking through the lessons of the Prosperity Circle. Let's begin with perhaps the most essential practice that will not only launch you onto your Path of Prosperity, but also, when done consistently, will help energize your ability to be great with money.

Prosperity Tip: To initiate immediate prosperity in your life, start the practice of Giving and Receiving.

Why is it a practice? Because most people think they know how to give and receive when, in reality, they practice only *one* side of this prosperity equation. You surely have a friend who gives you thoughtful presents, remembers your birthday every year, and who comes to your assistance when you need last-minute help. But try to give her (or him) something in return, a simple compliment or a surprise gift of her favorite music, and she deflects it by telling you, "You shouldn't have done that. It wasn't necessary." or "You don't have to spend money on me." You may as well give your gift to a rock because that friend has not learned how to *receive*.

Or maybe you have a friend who is expert at taking your gifts of many lovingly prepared meals, daily rides to the station, and occasional tickets to a concert, yet in all those times has never even acknowledged your thoughtfulness with a simple "Thank You!"

These situations illustrate that Giving and Receiving is an art form we can all learn better through daily practice. That is why our picture of the Prosperity Circle shows Giving and Receiving at the core of the circle. It is *the* most basic way to fuel and keep fueling a prosperous life. Cultivation of this habit alone can cause a major shift in your

reality. When you become Great with Money, you will know t.
son in your heart and you will practice natural acts of Givin,
Receiving effortlessly and daily. You will also realize how each   ⸌ᵣ
of the Prosperity Circle contains this basic principle. Before you start
your practice, here are some insights we want to share.

Giving Continuously

When you examine the Prosperity Circle note the flowing energy in
the center of the circle that fuels its success: the mutual process of Giving
and Receiving. Giving, as a principle for virtuous living, has been with us
for centuries and appears in many cultures and religious systems. In the
Christian tradition, Jesus' instruction to "Do unto others as you would
have them do unto you" is the impetus for many charitable acts. The
Muslims have Ramadan, a month-long celebration of prayer and fasting
that ends in Eid-al-Fitr, a time when they feed the poor and make contributions to their mosques. The Jewish religion speaks of tzedakah or acts
of charity. Traditional Jews give one-tenth of their income to charitable
causes. Within African, Hindu, and Buddhist traditions, the idea of giving extends to caring for others in the community at large through daily
acts of giving and compassion as well as during times of celebration.

The wonderful benefits of giving to others of your time, energy, or
money are many, including: new perspectives gained, feeling good,
and building a community of care for others, as well as giving back to
others in exchange for the rewards you have reaped. If appreciation
and gratitude are the *outflow* of feelings that can motivate a giver, love
and abundance are the direct *inflow* of feelings for the recipient. Think
how different our world would be if we each intended and delivered
a daily "gift" to others.

The Boomerang Effect—
What Goes Around, Comes Around

Those who are great with money understand the practice of giving (outflow) and receiving (inflow) in the world. What you give
out does return to you, just as when you throw a boomerang and it
comes back.

Prosperity Tip: Taking responsibility for perpetuating this cycle of giving and receiving not only ensures abundance for others but also returns it to you, increasing your own flow of abundance.

We have all had an experience as simple as opening the door or assisting someone with heavy packages, only to shortly thereafter receive the gift of a free parking space or surprise compliment. The saying "What goes around, comes around" reflects the interdependence between giving and receiving.

In our business, when we give referrals to people or support to business colleagues, we see our own business grow in turn. This may not be as a direct payback from the specific person we helped but as opportunities continuously flowing our way from unexpected sources.

A newly formed graphic design firm adopted a core business practice of making a helpful connection for every business contact they met. These introductions often did not relate directly to business for the design firm but did make a big contribution to their contacts. The connection might be a professional referral or an introduction that could lead to potential business opportunity for someone else. Each week at sales meetings within the firm, they discussed who they had helped and connections they had made for others. As a result of adopting a core business value of giving to others, the graphic design firm experienced dramatic growth in their business and within a short amount of time was competing with the biggest firms in the area.

Understand that we are talking about a gift to help others, not a gift in order to get something in return.

Prosperity Tip: When you make a genuine difference for others, without attachment and expectation of getting something in return, amazing prosperity will come your way. This is a true practice of Giving!

There are many aspects and benefits to this boomerang effect. When you focus on giving, there is also little room for self-absorbed focus on your fears or sense of lack. When you give to others, it puts you into proper perspective, generates appreciation and gratitude, and can even humble you at times. A magical cure when you feel unsure or fearful of your own direction can result from extending efforts to assist others, especially without expectation of anything in return. You will soon forget yourself and be uplifted by the simple act of extending your heart or kindness to others first, making them a priority before satisfying your own needs.

Giving also prompts you to decide how and to whom you want to give. Family and neighbors may seem obvious choices, yet how often do you actually stop and make intentional gifts to those not close to you? As well as money, giving comes in many forms: kindness, time, knowledge, and skills. As you build your sense of connectedness to a community through giving, you may begin to ask the natural question: Just how far does my "community of care" extend and how do I create ways to make a direct difference in another's life?

We were shocked recently to hear a news story of a bright, young Chinese boy who committed suicide on the railroad tracks when he was unable to come up with the money to pay for his books and small tuition fee for education imposed in his province. Other children, more wealthy, mocked his less-fortunate status. His own parents had both died and he had been raised by his grandparents who labored to assure an education for him. But when the crops did not bear as much and his family couldn't come up with the assessment, in shame and despair he chose to take his own life. The amount he owed was the equivalent of 26 U.S. dollars. The story says it all. We need to have not only intentions directed from our heart in our giving but also ears that can hear the cries from around the world.

The wheel of giving must always be turning. While the act of giving primes the pump for receipt of your own abundance, be wary of your motivation and intention when you do give. Find the place of authenticity within when you give. Know the difference between a heartfelt action and one motivated out of self-interest.

And remember, when you feel least like giving because of your own stress or fear of not having enough, paradoxically that is often the best time to give. We have found that generosity at those times puts attention on others and the joy of giving dissolves feelings of discouragement, lifting you out of your own narrow vision.

At one of our workshops, Sheree shared that after hearing us speak of *playing big* in the world to serve others, she was stopped by a man on the street asking her for money for lunch. Normally she would have walked right past him. Instead, she actually heard what he had to say—he washes windshields to make money for food. Today was slow and he did not have enough money for food. She proceeded to walk the man into the grocery store a half a block away. While others stared at her, she proceeded to take him to the deli counter so that he could order a sandwich. She bought the man lunch and gave him the change from the ten-dollar bill she used to pay. Sheree felt great about helping the man and walked home with a smile on her face. Later that evening she received a call from a relative who offered her a gift of $10,000. She is convinced that the two events (helping the man on the street and the monetary gift) are connected. We are too. Giving to others always comes back to us—although not always this quickly.

Giving is an art that people who are great with money practice each day. Your gifts can be as simple as a smile to the older person in the elevator, a compliment given unexpectedly to a stranger, an offer to bring in food to an elderly neighbor, or showing appreciation and encouragement to your child. Starting today, pause and make a list of all the gifts you can give. Be creative and make them simple gifts you can give right now.

Receiving Continuously

People who are great with money know that receiving is insepa-rable from giving. They are flip sides of one another. One begets the other, and for that reason, the practice of receiving is equally impor-tant. Have you ever directed a gift to someone and they deflected your gift with a remark such as "It was no big deal," or "You know we can't afford that," or "Thanks, but I really don't think I look that special"? Something in our culture seems to prefer minimizing our gifts when we receive them. It is not better to give than to receive—they are both equally wonderful!

How can you be more open to receiving and appreciation? A wonderful starting practice is to acknowledge your abundance by expressing gratitude daily. Each time you notice you have received prosperity in your life, whether tangible or not, speak your gratitude out loud or silently with a simple "Thank you." This practice cultivates recognition and appreciation of the gifts that are *always* coming, which sometimes we may fail to recognize. Without this attitude of appreciation and expectation of gifts, you can easily miss the opportunities and prosperity that appear daily for you.

Note that an expectation of receiving is different from an attitude of entitlement. Expectation of gifts trains your attention to look for and to see what the universe is offering and delivering to you.

Prosperity Trap: Entitlement lacks gratitude.
It is a state of demanding. If you still have trouble
differentiating, there is little, if any, joy when
you receive if you believe you are entitled.

When you truly receive another's offering, you often are humbled as you are graced with someone's generosity and expression of appreciation. And that is what makes you want to return the gift. When you truly have connected and fully received a gift, however big or small, your natural response is to give in return—though not always to the same person. Try to "pay it forward" by passing on a surprise abundance to someone you might not even know. The concept of simply paying for your toll as well as the toll of the person behind you demonstrates this. You can gift others unexpectedly when you see a need; then the wheel of giving and receiving keeps turning round and round. This is the simple secret of one of the deepest experiences of true abundance we can all have regardless of our actual financial circumstances.

Throughout the book we will remind you to keep this most basic wheel of giving and receiving turning constantly in your own life. To be great with money is to inspire others with this behavior as well as to energize the Prosperity Circle.

Prosperity Steps to Activate Giving and Receiving in Your Life

1. Establish a "Giving Account" and put into the account a specific percentage of your net earnings on either a monthly or quarterly basis. During the year, begin to figure out how to direct this money as donations that match your values and ideals.

2. Institute your own Great with Money Daily Giving Program. Practice giving a gift to someone each day. Your gift could be a tangible gift of something you have made, recycled goods, a compliment you always have meant to give, holding the door open for that neighbor you thought you did not care for, a smile to every elderly person you see on the street, or paying for the toll of the car behind you. Let your creativity go. Dream up how you can bring gifts into others' lives.

3. Create a Prosperity Notebook. On a daily (or at least weekly) basis write down at least five "gifts" that have come into your life in the form of opportunities, new friends, offers from friends and others, fulfillment of a dream or vision of yours (big or small), or whatever you perceive as something for which you are grateful. Make this habit of recognition of receiving and gratitude a part of your daily abundance check-in.

4. If you are having trouble understanding what you are receiving, explore your thoughts and beliefs about receiving in the forthcoming chapter on Beliefs and Focus. With a declaration such as "I allow and appreciate the abundance which flows to me daily" you can start to allow receiving in your life more noticeably.

CHAPTER 2

Clear Your Clutter

How to Unleash the Flow of Prosperity

The first step in the Prosperity Circle is to clear clutter in your life. This is a simple way to begin making significant progress toward being great with money.

Have you ever had the experience of cleaning and organizing your closet or desk and feeling an unbelievable sense of accomplishment and lightness? Possibly you had the experience as a young child of one of your parents threatening to throw away your toys if you did not clean your room. Your motivation level likely increased at the thought of your Easy-Bake Oven ending up in the trash, not to mention making your parents happy. Do you remember how good it felt to finish straightening up? Maybe you even took your mom and dad on a tour of your room to see your good work.

As adults our lives can be a breeding ground for clutter, both physical clutter (papers, investment accounts, etc.) and mental clutter (thoughts about what we should be doing or should have done).

Rid Yourself of Physical Clutter—All that Stuff

Paper clutter is one of the most common messes that occur in our lives. Statements, prospectuses, annual reports, tax information, and insurance documents are just some of the endless mail that pours in on a regular basis.

For some super-organized people, handling paperwork is a piece of cake. Each statement easily finds its home in a file or notebook. For others, papers pile high and cause incredible stress. And here lies the issue. Each time you stare at a pile of unopened statements or disorganized documents, whether you are conscious of it or not, a thought is running through your mind, "I really should do something about this." Or, "I hope there is nothing really important in that pile that I should be dealing with."

On a very practical level, mistakes often go uncorrected as a result of disorganization. Over the years we have seen examples of errors such as money being mistakenly taken out of the wrong person's account or of people being charged erroneous fees. It is up to you to correct these types of errors. If you work with an advisor, they might catch such mistakes, but you should not rely on them to audit your accounts.

Prosperity Trap: Most people don't realize how keeping clutter in your life actually limits your prosperity. Every time you worry about what you are not handling or what you should be doing you are not focusing on what you want to create.

Keeping the paperwork tiger under control may be as simple as getting a filing cabinet or a series of notebooks. If you are organizationally challenged, hire a professional organizer to get you on track. The fees that you pay this person might easily be recouped by their catching errors on a timely basis.

You may also have clutter in your finances—such as many accounts in many different places. Nina is a 54-year-old divorced woman who works for a large company. Prior to her current job she worked for a small medical practice and before that worked at a bank. She still has money in 401(k) plans at each of her former employers. In addition, she has four different IRA accounts, two brokerage accounts, and accounts at three different banks. All those statements drive her crazy, and Nina doesn't feel that she has an overall sense of her assets or her plan. In addition, although she knows she could and *should* consolidate her accounts, Nina is so busy with work that she has never made the time to do so. This is the time to bring in a professional. If you don't know how or what to consolidate, or if you don't make the time to do what you know you want to do, then hire a financial professional to help.

Clear Clutter Exercise: Here's a quick clutter-identifying exercise for you. It's an important but powerful first step in learning the Prosperity Circle. Scan your home or a particular space as you walk through it carefully and slowly. Notice what happens each time you look at items in your home, office, closet, storage area, or garage. Are you happy and comfortable when you see these items? Do they give you a sense of joy? Maybe you feel neutral. Pay attention to whether you feel discomfort or aggravation as you view or think about your various possessions. Do you have some idea that keeps voicing itself or do you feel your energy drained as you contemplate some of your "stuff"? If so, you've likely hit "procrastination pile," for example, the closet you meant to clean last winter or the desk you have always meant to organize. Take note because *here* are the key places to tackle on your first decluttering action.

Prosperity Step: After this review of your home or office is complete and you have an idea of places to start your decluttering, write down all the possible projects you have spotted. Then, from that list, pick the *easiest and smallest* decluttering task you can perform. Why start small? If you start small, you will complete the decluttering quickly and get immediate satisfaction from your effort. Now begin to notice any new events and surprises, which often start to flow when you initiate decluttering as a routine.

Rid Yourself of Mental Clutter—All that Chatter

Is your clutter less about dealing with paperwork messes and organization, and more about a real financial mess that you have yet to handle? Maybe you have a tax return that was never filed or a medical claim that was never made? How about an investment that went badly that you are still beating yourself up about? We call this Mental Clutter because you carry it constantly in your mind.

Prosperity Tip: Mental clutter can be a little subtler sometimes and perhaps harder to spot initially. How does it show up? Look for a repetitive problem that you haven't taken action to correct, like a recurring physical ailment for which you haven't scheduled a doctor's appointment.

This is the kind of clutter that stays in the background of your mind because it doesn't get resolved. It is often something you tolerate or are bothered by but make no steps to change. In short, you are mentally carrying a pile of things you tolerate.

For example, we often see people procrastinating on revising or creating their estate plan. Jennifer, a business owner in her late forties, shared that she was given drafts of a will and trust by her attorney months ago and has a few decisions to make regarding what would happen to her assets if everyone she currently cares about dies before her. Although this event is highly unlikely in the near term, her lack of decision holds up completing her estate plan. Jennifer said "every time I get on a plane or in my car for a long trip I worry about the fact that I haven't completed this." *Where thought flows, energy goes.* By not finishing this process, Jennifer is spending her energy on worry as opposed to freeing her thoughts to focus on what she wants to create for herself (more on this later in the chapter on Beliefs and Focus).

Some of the most disruptive mental clutter arises from unhelpful internal messages, whether these are from parents or other authorities, or possibly ideas from something you read or saw on TV, such as "Are you prepared for your retirement?"

Have you ever experienced repeating a phrase in your mind, recalled from your past or an old experience, that influences your behavior ("Never spend your principal," "I'll be a bag lady if I don't watch my pennies," or "Men are better at finance")? These are definitely areas of mental clutter to notice. The idea is not to blame anyone for your financial condition. Better to start the process of decluttering your own mind from the ideas and beliefs that limit your goal of prosperity. Your exercise for now is to just *notice* these thoughts without judgment. Simply begin to ask yourself whether these ideas serve you or cause unnecessary worry and limit you.

Prosperity Tip: Clearing out clutter can even save you money! If you are not an organized type in your financial affairs, you might not catch any mistakes such as erroneously charged fees, bank errors, or bad charges on your credit cards.

Clutter in your financial life may keep you from making smart moves to help move you closer to your goals. Here is an example:

Debbie, a successful corporate executive, at age 40 still had her mother listed as the custodian on several mutual fund accounts. Not only did she think about how she should do something about this every month when she received her statements (diverting her energy from more productive things), but having her mother's name on the account restricted her ability to make changes to her investments. She had kept these investments for years just because she didn't want to deal with changing the account to be solely in her own name.

By organizing her finances, Debbie was able to "create" more money to reach her goals. During the process of getting her financial house in order, she found $500,000 in stock she "forgot about" since the certificates were held in her safety deposit box, as opposed to her brokerage account. As a result of her planning, she is now on track to slow down at work and quit altogether if she gets fed up with her firm. Now, many of us will not be this fortunate to stumble across large sums of money, but who knows what we might find! Several individuals have found uncashed checks in their piles of paper. Maybe you'll find an old stock certificate, gift certificate, or something better!

Perhaps you know someone similar to Tony, who inherited a house full of furniture when his mother died. Some of the furnishings he put into his home and the rest he put into storage until he could decide what to do with them. That was ten years ago. For the past ten years Tony has been paying $200 per month to store things that he is not even sure he likes. This physical clutter is not only taking his mental attention (every time he receives the storage bill he thinks "I really should do something about this stuff."), but saps his financial resources as well. If that money had been saved, Tony would have accumulated more than $24,000 during the past ten years.

Clear Clutter Exercise: One of the most effective methods to start a clean-up of your financial house is to *regularly* remove any pockets of clutter. Schedule at least 30 minutes to an hour of decluttering every 30 days if you want to keep your life rolling. Start your Path to Prosperity with a thorough effort to toss out paper, objects, furniture, clothes, and even old ideas. Follow this practice and you will see and experientially learn more about how to make your dreams of prosperity thrive within the newly empty space you have created.

Richard shared with us that after hearing about this exercise he took on the challenge of cleaning out his life insurance files. Although very organized in most parts of his financial life and having a solid financial background (he has his MBA and had worked in banking for many years), these files were a mess. He did not really understand what life insurance he and his wife had or why they had it. He now realizes that this was a circular problem—the reason that he didn't "get it" was because he mentally resisted tackling the insurance paperwork, organizing it, and figuring out what was there. After cleaning out the clutter in the file and reorganizing it into a binder he reported to us: "I feel really good and I actually see the life insurance picture much better in terms of our whole financial plan."

Remember, the more you collect any kind of clutter, the more possibility of being stuck, and less opportunity for the energy of prosperity to appear in your life. You will leap out of a static place when you declutter, and you will never know whether the movement will be small or very large until you take this action. When you clean out your closet and pass on clothes to someone who will enjoy them more than you do, you create a void. Since nature abhors a vacuum, your closet will be filled with new and better clothes somehow, some way. In the same way, if you clean out your "financial closet" new and better finances now have more room to come your way!

A quick note about how giving and receiving (in the inner part of the Prosperity Circle) relate to decluttering. When you follow the Clear Clutter Exercises you often will end with giving away your clutter to others. This accomplishes another Great with Money principle sure to prime the pump for prosperity: continuous acts of giving and receiving. Your clutter can become a real gift in another person's life and a moment to practice generosity. In turn, you will experience the joy of receiving in the form of someone's appreciation for the gift and the well-being that comes from making a contribution, as well as definite, tangible surprises entering into the void you created.

Physical Clutter ("all that stuff") Exercise: Use the following questions to find key areas of physical and investment clutter in your life:

1. Do you have piles of unopened mail or papers that need to be filed?

2. Are you afraid to throw paperwork away (even though you are not sure you need to hang on to it)?

3. Is there a specific reason to maintain each bank and investment account that you own? Could you consolidate accounts? Do you need professional assistance to answer this question?

4. If something happened to you, would someone be able to step in and handle your affairs? Would they be able to determine what you have and where it is located?

Mental Clutter ("all that chatter") Exercise: Use the following questions to assist you to find key areas of mental clutter in your life:

1. When you make a decision, do you hear your parents' or other authority's voices repeating a message? What is that message they gave you about money? Did you receive messages about becoming financially independent? Were they scarcity-focused or prosperity-focused?

2. Are you hanging onto an investment solely for an emotional reason, e.g., it was Aunt Sally's favorite stock and you loved Aunt Sally? Look at the real reason that motivates you to keep an investment.

3. Is there someone or something you need to forgive about a financial matter or resentment concerning money you need to discard to clear your mental clutter?

4. Is there a decision you have been putting off making or one for which you continuously gather information?

Prosperity Step: Pick one answer to the above questions
and decide to take action to erase that
physical or mental clutter now.

Prosperity Steps for Clearing Your Clutter

1. Clear a physical space just for your records. Start small, with your desk or closet. Purchase a new filing system or record-keeping system. Visit www.begreatwithmoney.com for a guide on how long to retain important documents. Make sure to shred any documents you are discarding that have personal information. A good system will help you understand what's important. A system helps focus your attention. You'll change your energy around your finances just by changing your systems. And, according to many a story, you'll start to catch mistakes—yours and others'.

   Write down one mess that you want to clean up and complete it this week. Then move to your next item until you clean up all your clutter messes.

2. Make a contract with yourself to clean out the clutter in your home every 60 days. Give away what you don't need, recycle it to friends, and reorganize your cleaned-out space.

3. A powerful variation of the above: For seven minutes daily, take some action to declutter your space. Do this each day for a period of one week.

4. List five to ten unfinished, unresolved issues (make at least one a financial issue) you have been worrying about for 30 days or more. Pick one issue per week and take action to resolve it.

5. Come back to clearing clutter whenever you are feeling stuck or overwhelmed. This is a wonderful way to increase your energy to move you along the Prosperity Circle.

CHAPTER 3

Beliefs and Focus Make or Break a Dream

OUR BELIEFS ABOUT MONEY and the words we say to ourselves and others steer our money focus. They can either boost or seriously limit our options. Sonia's story reflects how ignorance of Beliefs and Focus—the next Prosperity Step—stunted her financial options and dreams.

The first thing Sonia said when we met was, "I've always been terrible when it comes to money. I've had credit card debt as long as I can remember—we always seem to spend more than comes in." A closer look at her financial situation confirmed that everything she said was true; she had amassed more than $50,000 in credit card balances and this number was growing. In addition, she and her husband had taken out a large home equity loan to bail themselves out of past financial problems.

Sonia did not know that she was demonstrating a powerful money lesson: *What we believe and say about money and where we put our focus directly impacts what we bring into our lives.* Sonia did not understand that if she fed her negative beliefs about spending and debt and focused constantly on what she no longer wanted, she would continue to get just that: more debt and a struggle with money.

When we learned more about Sonia, we found something else was also true. Sonia was amazing at bringing money into her life. She was a chiropractor who always had a full practice. In addition, she applied for and received research grants to investigate new healing methods. She also had family members all over the world sending her money to come visit them. Having money flow to her was a gift Sonia definitely had.

Once Sonia learned the important Prosperity Step about Beliefs and Focus, she corrected a negative belief and shifted her focus onto her money *strengths*, away from what she no longer desired in her life. Sonia saw she was, in fact, a fabulous money earner, yet in her mind she carried an old *thought,* the *belief* she wasn't good with money, and had borrowed quite a bit of cash from friends over time to support that belief. That negative money mind-set encouraged a system of piling on personal loans, which left her very unhappy about her financial affairs. She tossed out the old, limiting belief that she was terrible with money—an idea that unnecessarily limited her actions and choices, and she promptly began to pay off the loans, put her record keeping in order, and move forward in life recognizing she was fully capable of financially supporting herself.

The net result: Sonia not only felt more control around money, but her debt actually decreased.

What Type of Money Beliefs Do You Hold that Do Not Serve You?

Consider these three important factors as you explore and develop a more prosperous mind-set:

First: Your constant stream of money chatter (beliefs and words) impacts what you achieve financially. Your beliefs are the foundation for your financial success or failure.

Second: Notice where you choose to put your *mental attention*. Is it on the positives or the negatives?

Third: Design your life. Make a commitment to yourself to, at least once a day, deliberately design your money focus and your mind-set. Shift into your money positives and away from your negatives. This simple step will create a prosperity mind-set.

Your Beliefs DO Matter

Few of us know the prosperity secret that how we *think* about money and what we *say* about money directly impacts our financial reality. Tell yourself "I'm a bad budgeter" and watch what happens to your attempts to stay within a budget. Tell yourself "I'll never understand the basics about managing money" and watch how you mismanage and become discouraged over your finances.

For some people, the opposite happens. Tell yourself "I will create the extra money for that trip to Hawaii" and the money-making opportunities show up for you. If you say "I know I will be able to get the degree I have always wanted, because things always work out for me" and then direct your efforts toward that end, a scholarship opportunity might suddenly arise.

Prosperity Tip: What you *believe* and what you *say*
to yourself about money—intentionally and even
unintentionally—really *does* affect your life.
Your thoughts and ideas about money are the
main ingredients of the recipe for the financial feast
you do or don't prepare for yourself.

How Beliefs Seed Your Financial Garden

Here is how it works. Imagine that your beliefs are the "seeds" you plant in the financial garden you want to grow. As a beginning gardener in a real garden, you start by planting real seeds. While tending your garden daily, if you look around and don't feel so successful, and tell yourself frequently, "I don't have a green thumb. My mother was a terrible gardener. She killed all her plants." You are now also planting your *mental* seeds by bringing up past experiences and beliefs and starting to treat them as a truth. When your real seeds refuse to surface as small sprouts, you say, "Look at that. That seedling hasn't grown an inch," or "I knew I wasn't a gardener," and pile on even more negative beliefs.

Now, switch scenes and imagine you are a person who believes she can create an outdoor garden sanctuary that offers reflection, colors to gaze at, and scents to take in, as well as a beautiful place for dining outdoors. Nice thoughts! Each day, as you tend your garden lovingly you also plant mental seeds aligned with your beliefs: "What a beautiful garden! I can see you growing each day." You think to yourself, "I can't wait to look at my fabulous garden and share it with friends over a luscious dinner." Guess which garden and gardener might stand a better chance to flourish?

Here are a few real-life examples of how we "seed" our lives. A colleague once shared with us that all of her "rich clients were cheap bastards." When pressed a little further, and asked if *all* of them were like this, she said, "Yes, everyone I can think of." We marveled at what an interesting reality she had created for herself based on this belief.

To avoid being "a rich bastard" like her clients, she "successfully" created a struggling financial life where she has come out of semi-retirement to work full time to make ends meet.

For years, top coaches have embraced and used the techniques of mental preparation to get their elite athletes ready for competition. Athletes learn to give themselves consistent, positive verbal messages along with concrete visual images that depict all the required motions to result in a winning performance. The United States Olympic Committee has a full-time staff of sports psychologists working with coaches and athletes to improve their performance and master the mental skills for their sports. On their website, it states:

"Athletes can easily learn the basic mental skills such as imagery, goal setting, energy management, effective self-talk, concentration, mental preparation, self-confidence, and how better to handle the pressure of competition."

An Olympic swimming coach employed these "winning" tactics when he came to a local high school to work with the swim team. He spent the first half of the training session having the swimmers practice winning. Each teen would swim a length, practice hitting the end wall, looking at the clock, and reacting as they would if they had won the race in record-breaking time. He told them "It's hard to win if you don't know what it feels like."

This scientifically proven process of "seeding" success with your beliefs, words, and images not only encourages athletes' high performance during training but also leads to frequent success in competitions. Don't you think that most people could enhance their financial "performance" if they were better able to manage their mental mindset about money?

Prosperity Tip: Practice winning in your financial life
by deliberately choosing beliefs about money
that support your success.

Uncovering Beliefs Exercises: People who are great with money foster thoughts that drive towards a goal of prosperity. Your beliefs can *indeed* determine what you achieve along the Path to Prosperity. These exercises will aid you to uncover any limiting beliefs.

1. First, do some digging and look at your *beliefs* regarding prosperity. What were the subtle and actual lessons you learned about money? Take a moment to look back and remember your experiences. What did you see growing up? Did your parents both go off to work or was it just one parent? Did your parents fight over money issues? What did you hear? "We don't have enough money to pay the bills." "Go ahead, treat yourself. Life is short." Or possibly money was a subject never discussed in your family...even a mystery? Did you get positive and negative messages about money? "They're rich and they're nice." "Don't flaunt your wealth." "All rich people are cheap." Write down your observations and memories.

2. Now dig further, especially with any unpleasant financial experiences. Did you get passed up for the promotion you thought you deserved? Did you lose money in your 401(k) during a market dip and have yet to recover it? Savvy people commit to being curious about their money beliefs and ideas and how these thoughts influence creation of a prosperity dream. Start paying attention to *what* you believe and *what* you say about money. Just *notice*. Don't try to change yourself or beat yourself up. There is no right or wrong. It's just *how* you believe that you want to investigate.

3. Write down your thoughts about money for three days—whatever passes through your mind or lips so that you can begin to see what you actually do believe. Ask a friend about your comments about money. Listen for messages that might sound like these: "I can't go on that vacation; it's too expensive." "I'll never pay off my student loans." "This idea is going to make me a million." "Giving to others is better than receiving."

4. Practice winning with your money. Use a blank check register and put in a deposit that would be large for you: $10,000, $100,000, $1,000,000! Make up a financial statement for yourself with all the balances you would like to see. Remember to make not only your assets large but also your debts eliminated.

You may discover thoughts and beliefs that feel like bedrock—they are too much a part of you and possibly your upbringing to just abandon. First, realize you have already started to shift by becoming aware. Just recognizing your words about money is a significant part of the process; you cannot shift thoughts of which you are unaware. At the end of this chapter we will give you more Prosperity Steps for this area. Do them in the spirit of being an explorer.

Control Your Focus on Money Issues

If your attention falls frequently on fears around money issues—the "deer in the headlights" syndrome—and the beliefs flowing in your mind are largely negative, take note of the good news: You *can* take charge of your attention and you *can* shift your money focus! It is easier than you think using the tools we provide later in this chapter and throughout the book.

Prosperity Tip: You are in charge of what money beliefs
you focus on, as well as how much attention
you devote to those issues.

Discover Your Dominant Money Focus

Have you now discovered a thought or two that might limit or undermine your prosperity? Do you feel you focus too much on lack of money? Or do you live in a place of generalized financial fear and paralysis? We'll show you ways to change this. But, first, congratulations for your willingness to take an honest look! You have just achieved a critical awareness of your money beliefs and where you *focus* your attention. You have moved through a vital step within the Prosperity Circle.

Here is a simple example of how we let our minds instill beliefs unconsciously and repetitively focus on negatives instead of being in the driver's seat. Pretend you are driving to work in your car. During your commute the traffic slows considerably and you encounter an accident with damaged cars on the left side of the road. This scene troubles you even though there appear to be no injuries. You continue on to work and throughout the day your mind keeps replaying this scene. You are disturbed even more and are fearful as you anticipate your own daily commute. In this example your mind focused repeatedly on the original scene, adding even more dire possibilities to it. You seem to have no control over this situation.

Similarly, when looking at money issues, many people put their focus on a past negative experience, such as a loss in the stock market or an unhappy investment decision. You might even avoid giving your money issues any attention out of fear or resistance to the topic. Yet other people put their focus principally on positive ideas of the prosperity they want to create, for example a new business, a retirement destination, or a lavish trip to a foreign place.

Prosperity Trap: Focusing your attention on past financial mistakes or uncertainties in the economy is a sure-fire way to increase your chances of experiencing financial failure and also to increase your stress levels.

People seem to either put their money focus on what they *don't have,* or what they *desire to have,* yet others find great contentment by focusing on what they are *grateful to have* currently.

Prosperity Focus Exercises:

Let's examine where you put your money focus. Is it on past losses, future worries, a financial secret you have been keeping, a shopping trip you just have to make? Where do you want to put your focus? How much of your time do your thoughts dwell there? Jot down five places where you focused your attention during the past week. Did you look to the past, present, or future? What thoughts or images do you emphasize most or commonly return to when financial issues arise? Are they positive or less than positive? Write down all you learn.

Keep this list in a place where you can refer to it easily and each time one of these topics comes to mind or you are excessively focused on a negative thought, practice either of the techniques below:

1. **Cancel! Clear!** State "Cancel! Clear!" out loud when that unwelcome thought comes into your mind. That effectively tells the mind to erase that thought—just like hitting the delete button on your computer.

2. Use **Change the Channel,** which allows you to gain control of your focus. Intentionally shift your thoughts off a negative topic and onto another topic you prefer, just as you would change to a preferred channel on the radio. (These techniques are described more fully in the Prosperity Steps at the end of this chapter).

Practice these techniques for a period of at least one week. Recognize specific times when your mind gets cluttered with unhelpful thoughts. Take charge and shift your focus onto more positive and productive thoughts. A change in your money viewpoint can occur just that easily. This is also a great way to master a compulsive urge to spend when it appears to overwhelm you.

You Can Design Your Life

We are blessed with some remarkable tools to design what we desire. The problem is that we have often used these tools unknowingly all our lives. Quantum physics discoveries scientifically verify how our thoughts, words, and images create our world all the time whether we realize it or not. When you begin to notice what you think about money and where you focus your attention, you will step into your new job as the designer of your money reality. Step into your "designer shoes," see and own what you are creating with your thoughts and focus of attention, then shift your money ideas to what you *truly* desire. That's how you create the prosperity experiences you want. Recognize that if you created unwanted ideas about money, you have the power to change them too!

Avoid Being Caught in a LOOP
(Lots of Old Points of View)

A woman we know consistently said, while struggling after her divorce, that she needed a break. Guess what? She fell and broke her leg. This is a true story about how we create with our thoughts and produce unwanted results in our life. Do you ever catch yourself saying "I'd like a bigger home, but what if I lose my job and can't afford the mortgage?" Or other comments such as "I could do that… but what would people think of me then," etc. Pay attention to the ideas that initiate the journey on your Prosperity Path ("I would love to visit Bali") then are followed by a limiting thought ("BUT I don't have the money for the trip").

When we speak in this manner—one step forward, another backwards—it's like being caught in a LOOP (Lots Of Old Points of view). We deliberately create a wonderful idea and immediately take away its power with a remark often based on negative past experiences. When we tag that limiting remark onto our dream, we effectively cancel out the new dream. That is a LOOP! We created it. It cycles around and around in a circle without any sense of achieving. Your job right now is just to notice your LOOPs. Realize that our beliefs and words actually create our life—yet can backtrack and limit it at any moment.

Identify and stay out of your LOOPs. In the forthcoming chapter on Vision we give you specific tools to keep your prosperity dreams active and at the top of your list long enough to create your dream, or, alternatively, to create a Path of Prosperity (POP) that will move you forward.

Prosperity Steps to Take Command of Your Beliefs and Focus

1. Beliefs

a. Your Money Mind-set. Write down your beliefs and ideas in regard to money. What do you believe you are good at? Making money, record keeping, saving, etc.? What do you think you are bad at? Add to the list any messages you received or concepts you learned as a child from parents or other adult figures, along with the money ideas that guide you presently. Put down at least ten thoughts about money or as many as you can discover. If you think you are not talented overall regarding money issues, list at least five things you do well; for instance, pay my bills in a timely manner, use coupons whenever I can.

b. Beliefs Can Support or Block. Review your answers to all your money strengths and limiting beliefs. Check the entire list and put an "S" next to the beliefs that support or cultivate a prosperity mind-set. Next, examine which beliefs might hinder or block achieving prosperity. Note the ideas or words that limit or block your true desires with an "H."

2. Focus: Clear Out the Old or Unwanted

Using the list of beliefs created above, review it to learn next where you focus most of your attention and/or decide which areas disturb you most. Look for negative thoughts you would prefer not to have or ideas that pull you away from a prosperity attitude. Words such as "I'm not a good saver" or "I can't handle my finances." Notice when you are focusing on that limiting statement and then choose one of the following simple techniques:

a. After saying the words, immediately state "Cancel! Clear!" to tell your mind to delete that thought and then go on with your tasks. The more you practice this technique the more effective it will become. Remember, saying Cancel! Clear! is like using a big eraser to wipe out the negative thought and limit its ability to create in your life.

b. Alternatively, use the Change the Channels technique. When your attention focuses on a limiting idea, picture a radio that is blasting the "noise" coming from that limiting idea. Mentally walk up to the radio and change the channel. Intentionally shift your focus to a new channel with a preferred topic, one that you enjoy. This requires a small amount of willpower on your part but reaps a big reward. If you just play the game you will soon see how easy it is to switch yourself off a topic when it has become unproductive. This is a good tool to use to control desires to shop and spend.

If you care to explore your beliefs in more depth, consult our Resources section at the end of this book for suggestions.

3. Focus: Become a Designer

a. Focus Yourself. Make a list of five specific items concerning money (or other items) on which you put your attention last week. Then make a list of five specific items on which you would like to put your focus. Where do you desire to go on your Prosperity Path? Just become more aware of your focus and thoughts.

b. Give Yourself Lavish Abundance—Daily! This is a personal favorite of ours because it will bring abundance immediately into your life and shift away from negative beliefs and focus. Say to yourself every day: "I expect lavish abundance in every aspect of my life, specifically today. I expect, recognize, and accept lavish abundance. And, I am grateful for it." Pretty simple but we practically guarantee this one. The trick is *to say it, feel it, and mean it*! Notice if you contradict yourself internally by saying "Yeah, sure." If so, just use Cancel! Clear! or Change the Channel techniques to keep yourself out of a LOOP and start over.

Now sit back and expect the abundance to appear. Remember, the other part of your job is to *expect it, recognize it* and *accept it* when it occurs (in whatever form), and to *speak your gratitude* for it when it arrives. Let us know your success stories with this one!

When we started expecting lavish abundance, magical things started to happen. First, business increased. Then all sorts of fun things happened as well: We were consistently upgraded to suites when traveling, daily "gifts" showed up, and more. When we teach this technique at workshops people report back an immediate increase in winning raffles and drawings. One workshop participant reported back that after she started expecting lavish abundance in her life she was given the opportunity to buy the building that housed her business. She shared that she was tired of worrying about money and, focusing on lavish abundance, decided to buy the building. This has turned out to be one of the best business moves she has made. In addition, the income from the building is a key part of her future retirement plan.

4. Use a Token Reminder

Put a prosperity reminder in plain view. Find a totem or a coin or a small rock with a special word on it—how about *prosperity*? Keep it with you at all times. Put in on your key chain or in your pocket. You can really have fun with this by creating an altar, or use feng shui, or a favorite spirit symbol for wealth in your home. You might carry a reminder of prosperity such as a large-denomination bill of play money in your wallet. Actor Jim Carrey held a check for $1 million payable to him in his wallet for years until that money dream manifested. Whatever works for you is what counts. Use your symbol as a constant reminder of what you want to create. Meditate upon it.

5. Take Charge of Your Negative Past

First give up the Same Old Story (SOS) you carry around. We all repeat some major unpleasant incident that occurred in our life—the money lost in the stock market collapse, the ex-spouse (partner, friend, etc.) who cost you plenty and you've never recovered. Listen for the stories you drag around and tell to others. You discover them by being willing to hear your repetitions. These are real events we do not want to belittle; however, telling an old story, especially one that features you as a victim (the SOS part), dragging it around into the present all the time, limits your ability to create a *new story and new prosperity experiences.* Look at it as a form of mental clutter that you are especially attached to. It's like a proud, old battle wound you carry even though it was likely a painful event in your life. So, just exercise your power to STOP IT! next time you are tempted to tell it. Remember to be loving with yourself. Tell yourself you want to create a new story, get rid of old baggage, and provide room for what you want to create *now!*

CHAPTER 4

Create Your
Prosperity Vision

NOW THAT YOU HAVE LEARNED the first two steps of the Prosperity Circle, it's time to learn the secret of how to activate your dreams. This chapter will teach you how to successfully design and picture your dreams so that you can *immediately* launch your journey onto the Path of Prosperity.

In the traditional financial planning process, a client is often asked "What are your dreams?" or "What is your vision of what you want?" or "What are your long-term goals?" Some people are stimulated by these questions, while many more freeze and become intimidated or paralyzed. They feel they *should* know the answers to these questions, yet the answers often feel elusive. If thinking about your goals or dreams for the future causes any type of anxiety, know that you are not alone. Unless you were blessed by growing up in a learning environment where you were encouraged to define and pursue your dreams, and supported in how to do so, you might not know where to start.

To launch yourself on the Path of Prosperity, you need a clear vision of what your dream is—what it will look like when you are really living it. Our preferred definition of Vision is "the ability to think about or plan the future with imagination or wisdom." In this chapter you will learn how to design a Vision that fits *your* life. A well-crafted Vision springs from within and inspires, motivates, and sustains you unlike those adopted from external sources. Throughout this chapter we interchange the words Vision, Picture, Dream, Prosperity Vision, and Goal. Use any word you feel comfortable with as long as it refers to an idea that *you* create, one that originates from your deepest desires.

First, we want to share a story of how Monica developed a vision, which transformed over time into a bigger vision and ultimately lofted her onto a happy new career path. Monica moved out of a corporate middle management job that had limited room for career advancement. She decided to take a job in the nonprofit world, seeking a shift more in accord with her personal concerns. The new position gave her time to reflect on the value of her past work experiences, get a new perspective, and reignite a desire to finish up her education. Monica then formed a clear vision of her future, one where she saw herself returning to school, finishing up college, and starting her own business. This vision was strong and enduring enough to motivate her to return to school after investigating and planning how to balance school financed with part-time work.

The return to school brought Monica unanticipated joy and success in academics and exposure to two courses: pre-law and interpersonal communications. As a result she became inspired to form a *new* vision: that of becoming an attorney, one with corporate experience with a desire to deliver values and service to people in a uniquely caring way. The proper nurturing of this vision carried Monica all the way through law school, graduating to provide legal aid service initially, and then moving into years of a successful law practice. We think Monica is a great example of how a small vision that stirs you to the core can lead you down a continuous and joyful Path of Prosperity.

Another grander form of vision was at work in the life of Nelson Mandela, whose words "The struggle is my life" became the mantra for sticking tenaciously to his vision. He spent 27 years in prison during which he became the most widely known figure in the struggle against apartheid. In prison Mandela never compromised his political principles and was always a source of strength for the other prisoners. The core vision that sustained him for years was of a democratic society with blacks and whites living harmoniously and having equal opportunities.

Following his release from prison in 1990, his switch to a policy of reconciliation and negotiation helped lead the transition to multiracial democracy in South Africa. Since the end of apartheid, he has been widely praised and ultimately was graced with the Nobel Peace Prize for his long-term vision come true.

As in the definition of vision at the beginning of this chapter, both these stories portray people who coupled the wisdom of life experience with imagination to project and plan an ideal vision of their future.

Vital Ingredients for a Vision Come True

The prior stories show that to claim a successful vision you require:

1. A Vision that brings you *joy*

2. A Vision aligned with your *values*

3. A burning *desire* to see your Vision become a reality

45

Joy Fuels Your Vision

A key element of a successful Vision is that it elicits Joy when you contemplate and begin to play with it. It is the deep awareness that "This is right for me and it feels great!" It has to "ping" inside you. So after the dream idea is birthed ask, "Does this picture bring me joy? Does it ping for me?" Remember, focus your dream on what you desire—not upon what you don't want. For example, a dream that envisions "My assets are continuously growing" brings you an ideal vision versus "I do not have any debts," which still ties you to the notion of debt. Lean into and focus on a vision that brings you joy.

Nick had a vision to be in better physical condition. He had struggled with his weight for years. When he thought about diets and exercise he felt anything but joy. While complaining to his friend Alex one day at lunch, his friend said, "Every year I ride in a 198-mile bike ride that benefits a children's hospital. Why don't you join me? We could train together, raise funds for a great cause, and you would get into shape!" Nick loved the idea. This adjustment to his vision was exciting. He continued to train and completed the charity ride with Alex. Nick had never accomplished this type of challenge before and had never imagined that he could feel such joy from a physical activity.

Prosperity Tip: Your strong desire, activated along with deep, personal joy, combined with what we will call universal energy, ultimately delivers what you desire. If desire and joy are absent, it is unlikely you will create and, more importantly, sustain your vision.

Support Your Vision with Your Values

Another important element is a vision aligned with your values. A value is a belief, a mission, or a philosophy that is really meaningful to you. Whether we are consciously aware of them or not, everyone holds a number of personal values; however, most people simply don't take the time to look at and examine what they value in life.

Prosperity Trap: A vision lacking accord with your values
is simply not *your dream.* A vision not aligned with
your values, or one determined by others
(such as your parents, partner, society,
or community), can be difficult to keep alive.

Yet a vision in harmony with your values helps you stay focused and brings you happiness. Most important, it will be realized exponentially faster and more effortlessly.

Corporations that clarify their visions in alignment with company values empower their workforce. Mary Kay, Inc. states its vision as "Enriching women's lives." This type of articulated vision empowers and inspires Mary Kay's independent sales force to work not only for themselves but for other women as well. This is a beautiful example of the boomerang effect of giving and receiving in action in corporate America.

The 3M corporate vision communicates the corporate values as follows: "3M's commitment is to actively contribute to sustainable development through environmental protection, social responsibility and economic progress. To us, that means meeting the needs of society today, while respecting the ability of future generations to meet their needs."

The exercise below will assist you to clarify the values that support your vision and will build the best foundation to design your dreams later in this chapter.

Prosperity Values Exercise:

Review the values list below. Circle or write down any values that feel right to you—ones that resonate with you (or attract you). Look for a quality or characteristic you admire or find inspirational. If the list is missing a value important to you, add it.

Next, put an asterisk (*) next to the ones you feel most strongly about. Last, list all the values you put an asterisk next to and rank them in order of the five most important to you.

Accomplishment	Dependability	Imagination
Resourcefulness	Accuracy	Dreaming
Independence	Security	Affluence
Education	Integrity	Self-control
Ambition	Energy	Intuition
Selflessness	Attentiveness	Enjoyment
Investing	Self-reliance	Availability
Experience	Joy	Simplicity
Balance	Expertise	Knowledge
Spirituality	Calmness	Faith
Learning	Stability	Career
Family	Leaving a legacy	Success
Certainty	Financial independence	Style
Support	Challenge	Friendship
Optimism	Teamwork	Charity
Freedom	Organization	Thankfulness
Comfort	Frugality	Perfection
Thrift	Community	Fun
Power	Wealth	Confidence
Generosity	Practicality	Winning
Consistency	Growth	Preparedness
Contentment	Happiness	Prestige
Control	Harmony	Privacy
Creativity	Health	Prosperity
Credibility	Honesty	Recognition
Decisiveness	Hopefulness	Relationship
Love	Discipline	Gratitude
Logic	Humor	Passion
Perseverance	Reputation	Wisdom
Flexibility	Reliability	Kindness
Making a difference		

Your Top 5 Values in Order of Importance

1. _____

2. _____

3. _____

4. _____

5. _____

Now consider: When you think about your financial life do the same top five values appear?

Keep Your Vision Alive with Burning Desire

We all are blessed with an incredible power to create what we desire in our lives. Unfortunately, often we have lost contact with our power. Even if you believe that universal laws or faith are an ingredient in your success, each individual plays a vital part in manifestation of his or her visions.

Prosperity Tip: The effort to propel a dream comes foremost from you—*you are the source of your dreams and you hold the power to carry them to fruition.*

All visions start with a thought based on your desire to create and maintain your dream. Only you know what you intend to create, only you can envision exactly what you want, only you can engage all your senses to bring it into life, only you can feel what your dream will deliver, only you can walk the steps to achieve and finally realize it. Although we often receive support and encouragement from others to obtain our dreams, it is your personal motivation to do what it takes that fuels the process. In the next chapter we will cover specific Action Steps to bring your dreams to life, and your personal drive is a key ingredient. When you get in touch with your real desires you also find lasting fuel for and commitment to your vision. Always ask yourself "Do I really want this dream? Enough to stick with it whatever it takes?"

The Formula to Create Your Successful Vision

Here is our strategy—the Great with Money Prosperity Formula— a sure-fire method to move you along the Prosperity Circle and create more abundance and prosperity in your life. Now you can immediately embark upon a path of clarity and create a complete vision. When you find an inner vision and move toward the best expression of that vision in your own life, your happiness multiplies along with your positive impact on others.

Now that you have identified your top five values in life you are ready to initiate your personal Vision by using the Great With Money Prosperity Formula. Here are the four key strategies needed to create a dynamic Vision:

1. **Think** What You Truly Desire—this is the beginning, intentional seed of what you want to create and what honestly inspires you;

2. **Mentally Picture**—envision in your mind your entire dream as if you were experiencing it in the moment;

3. **Feel aroused by that picture**—especially all the *joy, desire,* and any sensations it elicits for you; and

4. **Speak** the vision in a brief, simple sentence packed with clarity and your power to make it happen.

Now let's look more closely at how these strategies for Visioning will work for you before we move into our Vision Exercises:

First: THINK

Plant a mental seed. Begin to think about what you intend for your prosperity dream. The process always kick-starts with a mental seed about what you most desire and want to create. The idea may be simple, something you would like fulfilled today, or it might relate to a longer-term idea. It is important to plant a seed about what you DO want, not what you DON'T want, e.g., "I am healthy and fit" versus "I am not sick." Or, "Money flows easily or effortlessly" as opposed to "I stop losing money in my business." Let your seed ignite your desire. It is also important to develop your thought seed as if it was happening in the present...right now, already created, not in the future. For example "I *enjoy* financial security." As opposed to "I *will be* financially secure."

It is not uncommon for people to be unclear at times about what they desire for themselves. To gain clarity on what you desire, visit No. 3 under Tips for Using the Great With Money Prosperity Formula at the end of this chapter to help you get started.

Second: MENTALLY PICTURE

Next, begin to use your imagination to create a comprehensive picture of what you desire. Imagine yourself in the picture and actually see the events you desire happening in the present moment. Pretend you are creating your own movie and see yourself living your dream. Relish every aspect of your vision. If it assists your visualization process, write down all you envision. Write extensively on every aspect you see and imagine happening; include as much detail as you can. For those who have trouble creating mental images in your mind's eye, you might first complete No. 4—the imagination warm-up exercise—in the Tips for Using the Great With Money Prosperity Formula later in the chapter.

Tracey always dreamed of having a corner office with lots of windows. She saw this as a symbol of career success. When she decided to change her career and aspire to a higher professional level she continued to see a beautiful desk overlooking floor-to-ceiling picture windows. Eventually Tracey left her corporate consulting job to start her own business. Five years into her self-employed life she moved into new office space. One day she looked up from her desk and realized that she had the exact corner office that she had pictured when she was leaving her former job.

Third: FEEL

As you engage in all these steps you need to actively feel your prosperity dream. When you envision it, put *all your senses* into the picture. Be inspired by what you have created! Here is the part where your desire and joy and values really come in. Make the vision "ping." Activate your entire sensory palate along with your visual imagination: Notice the sounds of the scene you are living, see colors, sense smells, taste it, and allow your emotions to blossom to positively support your dream. Feel the joy of having and living your dream. Add others into your picture. When you do the exercise, which follows, spend time meditating on and luxuriating in your creation to make it complete.

Valerie had run several marathons, and although she finished and was proud of her accomplishments, she suffered tremendous physical pain after the races were over. She decided to envision a successful marathon starting from her training all the way through her post-race recovery. As part of her visualization process she felt the excitement to finish and the pride of her accomplishment, as well as her body feeling fit, strong, and healthy. Her deliberate, clear, and specific visioning, including the actual feelings of her dream, enabled her to finish the next race in her fastest time ever (beating her time from 15 years earlier) and feel better than ever. Although your vision might not include a physical component, actively feeling your vision is a crucial component.

Fourth: SPEAK

Speak your creation out loud. Begin by speaking about your vision out loud as though you are already experiencing it. As you are talking out loud about your dream, include how the ideal of this dream looks and feels for you. Then take the power of these images and feelings and develop a brief, positive, simple statement of your vision. Put it in the present tense. Say it out loud until you feel you really mean it. As you have learned previously, words do create and are a vital part of the process. Your voice—added to your thoughts, pictures, and feelings—is the final activating power step. Putting a voice to your dream brings your commitment forth and empowers you. This step tells you and the world what you intend to create so that you can successfully attract all you desire. Speaking your declaration also allows you to notice any wavering of conviction. If you become aware of any doubt, take immediate steps to move beyond any hesitancies or discouragement in your voice by repeating your vision until you are convinced. If you are having trouble with interfering negative beliefs, go back to the chapter on Beliefs and Focus. Remember the techniques of Cancel! Clear! and Change the Channel when discouraging thoughts arise.

Valerie, our marathon runner, stated her vision as "I train for, run in, and recover from the Chicago Marathon with joy, easy camaraderie, and good health." This declaration included all of the components that were important to her.

This formula of Think, Mentally Picture, Feel, Speak is wonderful to share with children. One night before he went to bed, Debbie's son Ben recited what he was grateful for to his mother, as he did each night (we will discuss the power of gratitude later in the Prosperity

Circle). He smiled and said, "I am grateful for our little cat, Checkers." Here is the thing: they did not have a cat and certainly not one named Checkers. Ben was thinking, picturing, feeling what he desired most *and* speaking about it as if it were already present. So here is how that story ended. Debbie had focused on what she did not want (a pet and the accompanying responsibility) while Ben was clear about what he did want (Checkers the cat). The end result...no cat...but not surprisingly, a dog joined the family soon after. Debbie was very careful after this to only focus on what she *desired*!

In sum, the Great With Money Prosperity Formula to create your vision is: **Think/Mentally Picture/Feel/Speak Your Dream.** Now that you have the Great With Money Prosperity Formula, let's move to the practical exercises on how to use this information and start visioning in your life.

The following visioning and meditation processes can be used on *any* dreams you want to create in your life—large or small, prosperity visions, or others.

Vision Exercise One: Vision for the Next One to Two Years

1. Start by making a list of the dreams you want to realize within the next one to two years. For example, that trip to the Bahamas you want to take next winter, or the new fuel-efficient car you would like to have within 18 months. Make a list of ten things you would like to create in your life within the next two years.

2. Now, from that list, select the *one* goal that inspires you most and that you *intend* to create—look for the feeling of joy and desire as you pick the one you are drawn to most and make certain it accords with your values. You will use this dream seed in your next Self-Guided Meditation Exercise.

Note: Whenever you desire, you may continue your vision work by repeating Vision Exercise One yet expand out in time. Imagine your vision for the next 3 to 5 years, then 10 to 20 years, then 50 years, and then 100 years. See what comes up and how it feels to have a vision for your lifetime and beyond. That's a fun Great with Money perspective!

Vision Exercise Two: Self-Guided Meditation for Vision of One to Two Years

Find a quiet, uninterrupted space for the next 15 to 30 minutes. You may put on some soft background music if it will facilitate the process for you. We recommend you do this exercise sitting up instead of lying down to create conscious dreams as opposed to dozing off.

Read through the next four steps before you start to guide yourself through the process at your own pace. It is important to continue this meditation until you feel complete. Your meditation should allow you to thoroughly explore, envision, and enliven your vision. Have fun with your imagination and all your senses. Take your time!

1. Gently close your eyes and take several deep breaths to relax fully. Picking your favorite dream from Exercise One, begin to feel how you would actually live out that vision. Imagine it has arrived and you are in the present moment experiencing all it offers. Feel the joy of having achieved your dream. Begin to open up all your senses.

2. Start to expand your mental picture. Picture your dream by adding colors, sounds, smells, music, or people who are there with you. Add any details you want to enlarge the vision: what you are wearing, your emotions as you walk through the vision. Feel it and see it to the best of your ability. Linger and enjoy. Act as if you have realized your dream with all the joy it brings right in this moment.

3. When your vision feels complete, take time to write down in a journal any details you choose about this experience. This will assist your recall and inspire you when you revisit these memories. You may also choose to speak about your pictures out loud, recreating your experience of the images just as you saw and felt it in your meditation, as though the dream were happening now.

4. Now craft a simple, brief, present-tense statement that expresses your vision fulfilled. Take your time to word it. Write it down and make it right for you. Any statement needs to be believable to you. *You have to invest it with all your thoughts, dreams, and feelings.* A

statement crafted to just sound good to others will not work. Your heart must connect with your vision and feelings simultaneously to fully empower a simple declaration. Use a statement filled with punch, such as "I have a romantic, fun-filled Hawaiian vacation." Or "I have my own business with an abundance of clients." A short declarative statement works best. Your statement has to inspire you when you see it and evoke for you all the joy and desire and feelings within your meditation. Don't be concerned at this point *how* you will create your dream. We will help you with this in the Action Step of the Prosperity Circle.

5. Next, say it out loud, slowly, five to ten times with all the belief and enthusiasm you can muster. You should feel your enthusiasm and energy growing with each reiteration if you have picked the right statement. Make changes in the statement if you feel the need to and repeat the new one as before. Say it loudly and proudly always! Voicing your dream by talking about it with supportive people truly helps to instill power in the vision and to create it.

6. Each day begin by stating your declaration out loud and lingering visually and emotionally on your inspired vision until your joy and desire appear. You can also visit your journal to recollect details, or add more if you want. You can even sing a song or play music that triggers your vision. It is your job to inspire yourself daily with this vision. Keep it going. Keep it moving within you always.

Tips for Using the Great With Money Prosperity Formula

1. As you begin to create your dream of a prosperous life, realize you are practicing and learning how to use the formula. If you find it easier, make your initial vision a fun, light-hearted one or a smaller dream. For example, start with a simple vision of something you want just for today, or this week, that would make your everyday living better, such as a parking space whenever you needed it, or a bus that will always arrive just in time for you, or always arriving effortlessly and on time for all your meetings.

   Remember to be very clear in your vision. You don't want just a great parking space; you also want to make sure that it is a legal parking space!

2. For those who want to jump into the bigger vision, first look at what you deeply desire. Take the time to go inside. If, for example, you choose to focus on the realm of finances, do you want to be stress-free? What else do you desire? A bigger home in two years? To start your own business and have income flow effortlessly? Do you want to take a special vacation with family or friends? Do you want a new car? Do you want to quit your current job and do work to clean up the environment? No matter what your vision, start with your desire and your joy as you plant the beginning seeds of thought. Then move into a more complete vision. Remember a Vision needs to align with your Values. It will create faster and with less effort when you are attached to it and it makes your heart "sing."

3. Sometimes people tell us that they have trouble defining their vision because they do not know what they want. It's really okay to not always be clear about what you want. Please don't allow that to stop you from getting to a dream. There is another way. Here's what to do. Get out a piece of paper, or better yet a journal, and put down at the top of the page the following question: *What is important to me?* Now, just start answering that question by listing all that comes into your mind. When your list is exhausted, review it to see if anything jumps out or whether an idea repeats itself. Take that idea (or just start with the first item on your list and work through it) and ask again: *What is important about that idea?* Keep going on this list until you work further and further down to your core desires. They will surface! This is a great way to help clarify what you really yearn to create. Once you have found a dream nugget through this journaling, take it through the meditation exercise in this chapter to help you expand on it further.

Prosperity Tip: People often have a *belief* that they do not know what they want but, when encouraged to do more exploration, the answer is really always there.

---

4. Imagination is an essential ingredient to spark any vision, and some people are just natural visionaries with active imaginations. Do you have a friend who walks into an old house or apartment and almost

immediately sees how to put a new look into place? Many of us, however, are a bit "vision-challenged." Here are a few pointers to get you started with a vision warm-up exercise. If your mind does not normally leap to images, it may just need some coaching.

Imagination Warm-Up Exercise: Your Perfect Private Place

You are going to design your perfect private space. If you prefer, you may start by gathering pictures for inspiration (go to "a" first) or move directly into the imagination exercise (go to "b" first).

a. Give a visual boost to your imaginary private space by first exploring images in magazines or favorite sources. Cut them out and paste them on a large poster board, journal, cardboard surface, or just collect them. Use these images to spark your leap into imagination and to help create your ideal vision of a private space. Add inspiring words or paint on your board with colors. Add textures with fabrics, pebbles, etc. Keep adding to your poster or journal as you get more inspired. Add more rooms if you want. This is your private space—ideal space. Imagination is really all about play so no censors are allowed! When you are ready, use these powerful pictures to launch a visit to your ideal private space by following "b" below.

b. Read this exercise first, then close your eyes and begin. Take as much time as you need to take this imaginary visit. A good part of this exercise lies in the *belief* that you have an internal camera.

Picture yourself in your safe, private space. If you have gathered images, you will simply drop into those images. Pretend you have an internal video camera filming all that you see in the space. Start an imaginary walk around your private space and notice what you see. As you walk and look around, begin to feel what you might desire to make your space more pleasurable, safe, and happy. Whatever you are missing, use the magic wand of your imagination to bring that item into your space. Now invite in your other senses: smell, sounds, colors. Add other items you need to feel comfortable and content. These might be books, food, music, furniture, a view, pets, or landscaping. Now sit down and rest in a comfortable spot and visually savor what your imagination has created. Feel yourself in this space and know that this place exists just for you and will always be available and filled with whatever you desire by using your imagination. Realize that you can start to design any dream with a leap into your imagination. Visit this private place often in your mind to make it *real*!

5. Play big! How can you make a difference in the world? How is your vision giving to others? Remember the importance of the Boomerang Effect. Change often begins with an individual vision. Starting in 1976 a Kenyan woman, Wangari Maathai, led a campaign called the Green Belt Movement that simply encouraged women to plant trees across all of Africa to slow deforestation. Today more than 20 million trees have been planted. The movement expanded to include projects to preserve biodiversity, educate people about their environment, and promote the rights of women and girls. In 2004 Wangari Maathai won the Nobel Peace Prize for her vision and the transformations it brought!

6. To expand your vision more fully, it sometimes helps to create visual images on a poster board or scrapbook, or to write out your vision in a journal. Cut out images from magazines that visualize your dream and paste them on poster board or in a journal to create your own "Prosperity Picture." Then inspire yourself daily with these images and writings. Add music or create a dance to further express the vision. Explore all your senses during the visioning and remember any that trigger your vision. This step allows you to embrace the feeling of what you are creating and to clarify your vision.

7. To continuously empower your dream, speak about it daily using a powerful declaration that expresses the prosperity dream you desire, as though you have achieved it already. Use present tense and keep your statement simple and declarative. "I am enjoying a fabulous, sexy vacation in Hawaii." Imagine and feel it. Now believe in what you say! Invest it with all your feeling. Connect your heart—through your words—to your vision. After a time you may not feel the need to repeat your vision declaration, but check in by speaking about it regularly. Note if your feelings, joy, desire, and values are on track and spurring you forward.

How to Keep the Dream Alive

Now that you have created your abundance dream, how do you keep it alive and assure it manifests? Remember, creating your vision is a continuous, daily process. You *do* need to show up each day and put life and effort into your dream by stating, picturing, and feeling your vision daily. This is the part where you continue to create by instituting small steps each day to keep the vision alive and constant to *attract* what you desire along the Path of Prosperity.

In addition to keeping your vision foremost in your thoughts and desires, now you must actively start to pursue your dream by designing an action plan. Your vision is not just handed to you gratis. You have dreamed your vision, put it forth, and many opportunities aligned with your vision are on their way right now. A solid vision helps to beam in these opportunities and give you focus. However, you have to pursue *actions each day* to forward your dream. The following chapter on Action will give you all the sure-footed Action Steps to begin to plot the daily actions to further your vision and translate that vision into a reality.

More Prosperity Steps to Create and Nurture Your Vision

Here are some Prosperity Steps to keep you inspired and moving in the right direction.

1. Find a talisman to keep in your pocket or desk or create your own ritual to refresh your conviction and remind you of your vision declaration.

2. Speak your vision declaration out loud daily and keep a visual or written reminder such as a Prosperity Picture board, journal, or a declaration to keep the inspiration going.

3. Share your dream with a Prosperity Partner, someone who will support and believe in you. Exchange words of support with other great with money friends. Share any doubts and seek encouragement.

4. Create a daily reminder in your PDA or calendar to keep you in focus.

5. Create your own *Abun Dance*—make one up and dance your prosperity dance to favorite music that inspires you. It's your dream and you can make it come alive any way you feel is right for you.

6. If you start to second guess and wonder if your dream will become a reality, revisit the chapter on Beliefs and Focus and use your Cancel! Clear! or Change the Channel techniques.

CHAPTER 5

Sustaining Your Vision

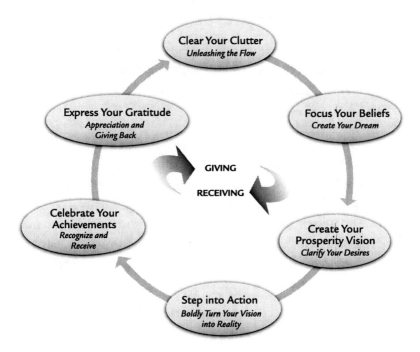

How to Stay in Play and Monitor Dream Breakers

You have completed your Vision and now the adventure starts. Here are a few realistic thoughts we want to share on how to sustain your Vision.

1. Recognize That You Are on a Journey on the Path of Prosperity (POP)

Sometimes a vision may create immediately, yet often dreams take time to create and you may find yourself on the Path of Prosperity (POP). If so, adopt the view of an adventurer who has embarked on a wondrous journey of creation.

Prosperity Tip: You *do* have the power and endurance to navigate your way until your prosperity dream fully appears.

Sometimes your dream may create immediately, and sometimes you are going to be an adventurer, arriving in new territory each day. Often dreams take time to create and so you will find yourself on the Path of Prosperity. When on the Path of Prosperity, remember to nourish yourself with ideas, supportive people, music, talismans, or whatever keeps you inspired. Repeat your declaration until you can confidently feel it creating within you.

2. Become a Good Navigator and Check Your Readings

a. Read and check the real data frequently

As you navigate your Path, recognize you will get new information that may cause you to alter your direction somewhat. But you are still heading for the destination of your prosperity dream. You may have to adjust your course a bit. Check your benchmarks and do not hesitate to check in with your advisor or supportive friends if you are thinking about changing course.

b. Be prepared for the "bad weather" of your mental clutter

Along the path you will need to monitor your intentions and thoughts to effectively navigate, deal with any discouragement, and keep on track with your vision. How to do this? What is the easiest way to do this?

Prosperity Trap: Learn to watch for and catch the moments when your thoughts and statements contradict your dream.

Notice any negative thoughts, appreciate them, and pull your attention off those "weeds" in your dream garden. Then focus on the positive aspects, restate your declarative statement, and reaffirm your joyful feelings and intention about your vision. In other words, restart your dream and your inspiration. We can all be dream creators, yet we can also be dream killers. Thoughts can come from within or from outside sources. Recognize if you are starting to fall off the track. Nurture your abundance vision. If you speak and think negatively of your own dream, you can sabotage it.

3. Practice Gratitude Along the Path

As you navigate your Path, recognize that you will get new information that may cause you to alter your direction somewhat, yet you are still heading for the destination of your prosperity dream. You may have to adjust your course a bit.

Most important, become alert to the blessings that are starting to flow to you.

Prosperity Tip: Part of your task is to *expect* your dream to create and to *recognize* all the ways your dream is starting to manifest.

As you go along on the journey practice gratitude for surprises which constantly appear. And always feel the joy of what you are doing right now. You are Great with Money, learning to use your power to create your dream. You can create any dream you believe in!

4. Get out of your LOOP (Lots of Old Points of view)

To ensure your vision is properly maintained, get out of your LOOP (Lots of Old Points of view). Realize that when you first state your vision declaration, you may not feel you believe it. This is a good awareness to have. When you make your statement to declare your vision, notice if your mind blurts something else just as you speak. For example, if your abundance affirmation is "I easily find parking spaces whenever I need them," pay attention if a voice inside then says, "No, I don't! I go around and around the block forever." This is an underlying belief that has just popped up contrary to your dream and now you are focused on it. Well, this can happen to all of us. We call this a LOOP.

Prosperity Trap: A LOOP occurs commonly when we want to take a new step forward, yet we have some old baggage of memories or hesitancy within us that shouts out "NO, you cannot" in some fashion.

You might feel as though you are starting forward, then pushing yourself backwards with a negative thought or focus that arises. Well, in fact, you are! There are several ways to deal with this natural occurrence:

a. When you become discouraged, seek out a Prosperity Partner or a friend whom you consider successful. You can often find inspiration by talking with and giving appreciation to another who is doing well on their path. Just ask how they keep on their path and make life work well for them. You will shift your attention focus off your own discouragement and renew your vision.

b. Also, do not hesitate to alter your declaration as you see fit. If there has been a change and new information flows to you that requires you to alter your vision declaration, then create a more specific statement or drop in a word or two that fits better. Go for it! You might want to change your statement from "I am a confident investor" into "My confidence in investing grows daily." The idea, however, is not to compromise your dream or change it constantly but to adapt it if truly needed. Then *do* stick with it until it creates. This is your vision. Have fun creating!

c. Another method is to repeat your declaration out loud and often or journal it until you *really* feel you are living and believing it. Realize that the more you have invested in thoroughly completing each of the prior fundamental vital steps (Think, Vision, Feel, and Speak), the more you will believe your dream can come to fulfillment when you state it. Go back to your Vision and Feel to empower yourself once more. It will happen!

CHAPTER 6

Stepping into Action

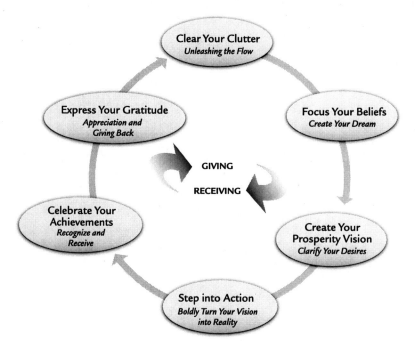

IF YOU HAVE BEEN WALKING along the Prosperity Circle with us, you have set the stage to create what you desire in your life. In the first step you cleared clutter in your life to make space to focus on your dreams. Next you gained awareness of your beliefs and how they impact your abundance. In the Vision step you planted the seeds for your picture of personal prosperity. Other methods of prosperity creation fail, because they stop right here. "Just believe and picture 'it' happening and presto...money and riches magically appear." Once in a great while it happens like this; however, the way to proactively turbo-charge your vision is not to sit by and wait but instead to be bold and take action on your vision.

The typical left-brain financial planning approach takes a cursory look at goals and objectives (typically ones that you are *supposed* to have, such as retirement and funding your kids' education). Yet it leaves out any look at what might hold you back from creating your dream. Nor does it help to articulate what you want to accomplish in the first place. Instead, the *Old School* (and most used) method of financial planning jumps right into running financial projections, implementation of investment strategies, and product choices.

We say stop! You need more *real* help. To create true prosperity you need to grow your Vision from the inside. Only then you will create an honest action plan that details the steps to move your dream into reality. A vision without action is merely a wish. Action minus a dream—*your* dream—leads to you living someone else's vision.

Vision *plus* Action that resulted in a dream come true is illustrated in Beth's story. Beth, a very successful partner at a consulting firm, was challenged in her career but began to feel that her creative inter-ests were being ignored. She was a star business generator and one of very few women partners at her firm. She was also a musician, com-poser, and singer with no time to pursue her more artistic interests. Beth began to clarify her vision of taking some time off to write and produce a CD of her music. She had always dreamed of creating a CD of children's music as a legacy for her three daughters. Realizing that she would work much better by concentrating her time solely on the music project, she pursued ways to make this happen. She estimated that if she had a full month to do nothing else but work on this project she could finish all of the creative work. If the actual CD production were not completed during this time, she would use the evenings, after work, if needed. Beth did some research and found a creative retreat center outside of Chicago where she could go to work on this project.

Next, she had to figure out how to take a month off from work. Although she had vacation time available, Beth wanted to reserve her vacation days for time off with her husband and three daughters. Would her consulting firm let her take more time off? Believing there had to be a way, Beth learned there were policy provisions for partners to take sabbaticals. Although no one had ever actually taken one, she saw this as a fabulous way to accomplish her goal. She approached the managing partner of her firm with the idea and, to her delight, she was granted a one-month, fully paid sabbatical. Her firm viewed Beth's sabbatical not only as a way to reward a key partner but also as a PR opportunity for the firm.

Next Beth looked at the financial implications of this project. As she had been a very good saver, the money to pay for the retreat center and the CD production was easily accessible in her saving account. Fortunately as her time off was paid, she did not need to plan for lost income. At the end of the one-month sabbatical, not only was the CD completed, but Beth returned to work rejuvenated and creatively recharged, not to mention an inspiration to her partners.

Beth went way beyond what most people do—just dream. Instead of wishing she had the time to produce her CD, she created the time, resources, and support to make her vision happen. Her dream of leaving a musical legacy for her children was realized. Beth's case verifies that goals developed with a strong foundation based in values and mapped out incrementally are realized much more quickly. The action steps to accomplish these goals then become quite easy and effortless (as in true magic).

Here is your step-by-step guide to create any Vision by designing your own Great with Money action plan. This template can be used for each goal you have, whether large or small. Remember, taking Action is crucial. Answering each question will help ensure you are doing what it takes to see your vision transform into reality. Start with the Vision you identified in the last chapter and take each of the steps in this chapter to develop an action plan and turn that vision into a reality. If you get stuck along the way, don't hesitate to reach out for support from a trusted friend, coach, or financial advisor. *You don't have to be an expert in each of these areas*—you just need to make sure you have all of the information to create your action plan.

A successful Great with Money Action Plan must:

1. Set a time frame to create the Vision

2. Determine the resources needed

3. Balance priorities and make choices

4. Use the right tools, tips, and tricks

Here's what we mean. Take your vision and start your action plan now with these steps:

Step One: Set Your Time Frame

When do I want my Vision to happen? What's my time span for the Action Plan?

The more specific you can be, the better your plan. For example, if you dreamed of taking your family to Europe for your 40th birthday, and you are 38, you have two years to plan for the trip. If you want to semi-retire early to go to Africa to work with orphans, pick a date you want to take your first break from full-time work. While analyzing other steps in creating your action plan, you may find that you want to change your time frame, and that's just fine—this is not cast in stone. Begin with a time frame and work towards it. Pick the date and write it down now.

Step Two: Evaluate Your Resources

1. What are the potential costs to create my vision?

This question may be very simple to answer or it may be complex. In Beth's example, she needed to plan for the tuition at the retreat center, the costs to produce the CD, potential lost income at work (which in her case was not an issue), and the potential lost career opportunities at her firm (to work on big consulting projects during the month off). Her list might look like this: Tuition and food cost? CD production cost? Lost income on retreat? Cost of risks: missed career opportunities?

If you are planning a big trip for example, research the costs in terms of financial resources as well as time needed to travel. If your Vision is longer-term, such as semi-retirement at age 53, then you might need to pull together more information to answer this question. The longer the term and bigger the vision the more moving pieces you will need to analyze and develop your action plan. One of the most important steps you can take to move your plan along is to make sure you are asking the right questions.

2. *Do I have the financial resources right now to make this Vision happen?*

To help answer this question, a look at your complete, current financial picture is invaluable. Once you have this overall under-standing of your finances, pursuit of your Vision will flow more logi-cally and effortlessly.

Here is the basic money information to gather:

What do I *own* (assets)?

What do I *owe* (liabilities)?

What's my *inflow* (income) and *outflow* (spending) of money?

3. *What do I own and how much is it worth?*

These are called "assets" in financial planning speak and consist of things like savings accounts, retirement accounts (IRAs, 401(k) plans, etc.), stocks, bonds, mutual funds, cash value of life insurance policies (the amount you would receive if you cashed in the policy, not the death benefit), investment real estate, annuities, home, cars, and collectibles. Make a list of all that you *own* starting with the most liquid (easily accessible) assets and finishing with the most illiquid (hardest to cash out). The easiest way to do this is to pull out your current statements (which should be easy to do now that you have cleared your clutter) or go online to find your balances. Put it all on a list labeled "What I own" (Assets). You can always go back and add on or omit as you find out more.

Many people don't have a good handle on all that they own. This is an opportunity for you to take charge and become more knowledgeable if you haven't in the past.

4. *What do I owe?*

Termed your "liabilities," these are your car loans, mortgages, school loans, credit card or other debt, etc. Write down the amounts that you owe, who you owe the money to, and what the interest rate is that you are paying for the privilege to borrow this money. Again, put it into a list labeled "What I owe" (Liabilities).

Now, put the two lists side by side and look at them. What you own *minus what you* owe *equals your* net worth. *You are shooting for a positive and growing net worth number over time.*

5. *What money flows in and what money flows out?*

To determine if you have sufficient extra cash flow currently coming in to fund your Vision requires you to know exactly what is flowing in and flowing out. Most people don't know what they are really spending on a regular basis. Even people who religiously keep track of their income and spending using computer programs rarely analyze this information. Invariably, when people are asked what it costs them to run their lifestyle they *underestimate* what they spend. Armed with solid cash flow information you will be better positioned to create an effective action plan.

a. *What do I spend? What is flowing out?* Look back at least 6 months to determine how much you are spending (12 months would be even better). The easiest way to do this is to pull out your check register and credit card statements. If you are concerned only about the total amount spent you can just add up all of the checks you have written and bills that were paid electronically. This is fine for many people. If you would consider yourself a better "spender" than "saver" consider looking more closely at the details of *where* you spend money. This will arm you with great information as you set priorities to move toward your vision.

Prosperity Tip: Using a software program such as Quicken or Microsoft Money to help you track your spending will make future planning much easier. These are terrific tools for both organization and Vision planning. These types of programs will assist you to automate the process of tracking your expenses. They can also make balancing your checkbook, preparing your income taxes, and keeping track of your investments much easier.

b. *What do I receive—What money is flowing in?* When asked this question, many people do not know their total yearly or monthly income. They don't have clarity on their salary or other money flowing in to their lives. For some it may seem crazy to be employed and not know what you are being paid. If you don't know your income, and feel like you should, stop right now and say "Cancel! Clear!" to that thought. So what if you haven't known your income in the past! Past is smashed. You are going to figure it out *now*. List all money coming in from all sources. Include: salary, bonuses, self-employment income, alimony, rental income, dividends, interest, gifts, social security, pensions, lotto winnings, etc.

Now, the moment of truth, look at your spending versus receiving (outflow versus inflow). Is the money flowing in *greater* than the money flowing out? Or is it the opposite: *less than*? To have the flexibility to fund lots of Visions you can start now to work toward becoming a terrific "saver." It will make a big difference in how quickly you can fund a vision.

Look at all the information gathered and ask:

6. *Do I have the current resources to create my Vision?*

If your answer is yes, congratulations! You can move on to creating your next Vision by returning to the chapter on Vision. If your resources cannot presently underwrite your Vision, proceed to the next step in your action plan.

Step Three: Balance Your Priorities and Make Choices

1. *How do I fund my Vision? By weighing choices and balancing priorities.*

Now that you have estimated the costs of your Vision and you have helpful details about your financial resources, you can begin to look honestly at and weigh your choices. Some Visions are simple to financially plan for and others are more complex and require substantial resources and time. Earlier we shared Beth's story about how she easily determined she had the resources to fund her creative sabbatical; another individual, Liz, needed more assistance to put together an action plan for her vision.

Liz is an obstetrician in a small medical practice. She dreamed for years about working in her practice for half of the year and volunteering with Doctors Without Borders the other half of the year. Although she had always lived below her means and saved well, she wasn't clear on what the real impact for her financial future would be if she took the leap and lived her dream.

When Liz looked at the impact of losing six months' worth of income and savings ability while volunteering, she realized that to create this Vision, she would need to make some major adjustments in her current and future lifestyle. It was not realistic to maintain her current spending level and reduce her income in half, so Liz looked for ways to make big changes in her monthly expenses. Her desire to make a bigger difference in the world was much greater than her desire to live in a luxury condo. She realized that if she was traveling for half of the year, the mortgage payment, taxes, and assessments were excessive. Liz decided to sell her condo and buy a smaller place that would be easy for her to "lock and go" while she was out of the country. She also decided to sell her car. As she lived in a major metropolitan area she could easily get around with public transportation and save the costs of gas, insurance, and parking. Based upon these adjustments, and with the assistance of her financial advisor, Liz determined that she could work part-time for the next ten years and then fully retire (based upon her reduced living expenses) if she desired. She also realized that none of these decisions were irreversible. She could start working full time again, buy a car, or move if she wanted to down the road.

When people retire, there are often trade-offs that are made. As financial columnist Terry Savage writes about saving for retirement in her book *The New Savage Number: How Much Money Do You Need to Retire?*

"You probably can't save *enough*—depending on how you define that term—so stop stressing over the dollar amount. Unless you win the lottery or sell shares in your company to the public, it's unlikely that you'll ever have more money than you can spend. Most people can always manage to increase their lifestyle cost to accommodate a rising income. It's a lesson in how wants can easily become needs.

Retirement is simply the reversal of that process. Unless you've saved enough, you'll shed those parts of your lifestyle that are no longer needed, and you'll focus on issues that suddenly become important, such as health and health care. The definition of *enough* will change as you age, and it won't be as painful as you imagine. The true definition of *enough* is a combination of savings, spending, and continued earning that will give you a reasonable retirement lifestyle."

2. If my homework on the above steps reveals I need more time and resources to fund my dream presently, how I will create the additional cash flow to fund the Vision?

If you do *not* have enough cash available *now* to fund your Vision, ask which of these four options you want to choose.

a. **Reduce Spending** and **Save** enough money for the dream?

b. **Borrow** money for the dream? Ask, am I comfortable borrowing to see my vision become a reality?

c. **Earn** more money and from what source?

d. **Take money from savings?** This choice might also require me to sell an investment to fund my vision. Am I willing to do that? And, if so, will I repay myself and when? How will that decision impact my other goals? Will there be a tax consequence as a result of the sale?

Consider these four basic options and make your initial decision on what your strategy will be: save, borrow, earn, or take from savings? In the next step you will have the opportunity to reassess that decision and get more advice if you choose.

Remember: The only way you can create more cash flow and savings is by spending less or bringing in more. In Liz's case, she decided to reduce her spending. Are you truly willing to make lifestyle changes to meet your goal? If not, you can instead pursue ways to bring in more money. Is it time to consider a part-time job or to talk with someone else who might consider lending you the money, or could you get a grant to fund your Vision?

If you decide to **take money from your savings or investments** to fund your Vision, be sure to look at the costs of doing so. These include "hard" costs such as possible taxes due as a result of cashing in an investment, as well as the "soft" costs of the lost opportunity in the investment as well as the impact on your other goals. For example, let's say you are a regular Rachael Ray. You just love to cook and your Vision is to renovate a kitchen. After doing some homework you determine the estimated costs to fix up the kitchen are $25,000. If you sell a stock worth $25,000 now that you originally paid $10,000 for, you will owe income taxes on the difference between what you sell the stock for and what you bought it for originally ($15,000 in this example). In addition, if you did not cash in this investment and the money was left to grow at say, 6 percent for 20 more years, it could be worth more than $87,000. If you also have a goal to retire at age 63, will using this money have too big of an impact on your retirement plan? Will the kitchen improvements add to the value of your home? (Make sure to be honest with this question—often people rationalize that they are investing in their homes. It's okay to want a nicer kitchen—just realize there may be trade-offs involved.) Ask yourself: is the joy that I will receive from this new kitchen worth it? You decide.

You may also consider **borrowing money** to fund your Vision. In the kitchen renovation example, you might consider taking a home equity line of credit to pay for the work. Again, remember to consider all of the costs and benefits. You will have a tax deduction for the interest on the loan, but you will also have a monthly obligation to pay this loan back. If you need help to calculate these options, consult a financially savvy friend or advisor.

Prosperity Trap: Be careful thinking that if you only had more money you would be happy and meet all of your goals. It is not what you bring in, but what you save that matters. If you are living beyond your means, it is better to look at how you are spending money, and if your spending reflects your true values, rather than fooling yourself into thinking more income will make the difference.

Time for some celebration! Okay, now give yourself a pat on the back and take a short break. You are more than halfway through your action plan. Relax, go back, and spend a little time, too, with your Vision. Return to your dream, and let it invigorate you or give it more life. Perhaps you have some details to add to it. Brush it up and savor the possibilities and the feelings you will have when it is realized.

Step Four: Gather More Viewpoints

1. *What else don't I know or has not yet occurred to me along this path?*

Now is the time to get a bigger picture on what you are planning. This may include bouncing your plan off a friend or bringing in other advisors. Having another supportive viewpoint on your plan will help make sure you have considered all of the options and opportunities.

Ask: Is there a smarter way to create my dream? Can I partner with others to create this? Do I need to find a financial advisor to help me to explore how to create more money or allocate my resources differently? Do I need to consider items such as tax consequences or benefits of certain kinds of saving or borrowing?

2. *Given my dream, am I on track? Do I need to give myself more or less time?*

What do I now see is a realistic time span for my dream to come to fruition? What part can I enjoy now? What will come later?

3. *What are my real priorities right now? Does my dream match the reality of what I truly want* **right** *now?*

Are there conflicts with this Vision which I need to examine? Are there trade-offs I am willing to make? Sometimes the challenging part of dreaming is when you have multiple priorities that seem to conflict with each other. "I want to move to another city, but my mom is in ailing health and I don't want to leave her," "I want to pursue my career, but my kids need me home now," "I would love to go back to school, but we can't take a hit in my income now." Often, there are ways to be on the path to your dream without sabotaging your other dreams.

Gina wanted to be closer to her family in Minneapolis but her husband's job required them to remain in Chicago. She looked into various options that would enable her to spend more time with her parents, including buying a small farm near Minneapolis. The thought was that they could visit the farm and connect with family on periodic trips. Her parents would also have a place to keep a horse and relax on the weekends. Her research revealed that this was too expensive a venture based on their current savings, and they weren't willing to borrow money against their home equity. This idea did, however, inspire her to think creatively about other options. They ultimately decided to give up having a car since they lived in a city with great public transportation. The money saved allowed them to help sponsor exciting family events in different cities that drew the family together happily and frequently.

4. *Do I need to reassess my goal or put it into smaller chunks?*

You may decide to adjust your Vision based upon what you have learned. You might decide to take more time to save for and complete your vision, or adjust your vision to be in alignment with your other goals, or even change your vision entirely.

Prosperity Trap: We caution you at this point not
to succumb to feeling discouraged if your resources look
slim and your dream far off. This is the place where
people can abandon their dreams. Do not use this as
an opportunity to slide back into old beliefs about
financial scarcity, or to resurrect old fears. This is the
place where many people find excuses not to reach for a
dream. Refer to the tools in the Beliefs and Focus chapter
as well as the Sustaining Your Vision chapter. They are
invaluable to move you out of discouragement and
stagnation back onto the action path.

Step Five: Tools, Tips, and Tricks to Achieve Your Vision

1. *What resources/people can I use to assist me in my goal?*

Guess what? You don't have to do this alone. People are so darn secretive about money that they rarely get the help and support they need to move ahead with their goals. Take some time to decide what type of advice and support will be most helpful for you.

2. *What kind of a financial planner do I want to be?*

Are you an involved self-manager who wants to become an expert or do you want to hire expertise? Do you enjoy doing research on your own, like minimizing expenses by educating yourself, and find investing to be a fun, engaging endeavor? Or do you like to focus on what you do best and managing finances is not for you? Do you look to others for assistance? What are your time commitments and financial resources for the task of organizing your financial goals? There are lots of software packages and financial calculators available for little or no cost, but you have to be comfortable and willing to do the analysis yourself.

3. Do I want to consult with or hire a financial advisor?

If you are putting off your dreams because you haven't made the time to figure out how to accomplish them, decide if it's worth it to pay an advisor to do the number crunching for you. If you want professional assistance, decide what type of advice will be most helpful and what you most want to accomplish with the relationship. For example, if you like running most of the numbers yourself and you just want to check in with a professional to make sure you haven't missed anything, then you seek an advisor who is happy to work on a consultation basis (just charging you to discuss and review what you have done). On the other hand, you may want to work with someone who will walk you through the entire process, help get you organized, and manage your investments. The clearer you are about the type of relationship and advice you want, the better the fit with the right advisor.

Prosperity Tip: When you interview professionals, be clear about what you want from them, how often you will meet for advice, and how they charge for their advice. Financial advisors can charge hourly fees, retainer fees, commissions on investment and insurance products sold to you, a percentage of your assets, or a combination of these. None of these fee structures is inherently good or bad, but it is crucial that you understand their compensation before you enter a relationship. If you decide to hire an advisor, make sure to find one that you trust and that feel you can work with to accomplish your vision.

Just as you would research and find a new doctor, one of the best ways to find an advisor that is right for you is to ask your other professional advisors (accountant, lawyer, etc.) and your friends who have had relationships with an advisor for referrals. You can also do research through professional organizations such as the Financial Planning

Association, www.fpanet.org. The Certified Financial Planner Board of Standards web site, www.cfp.net, has a lot of educational material that you can download or order to help educate yourself on the financial planning process, including how to choose a financial planner, with questions you can ask when you interview a professional.

4. Who will walk along with me as I build my dream?

People have as much trouble talking about money with others as they do about their sex life or death. We can talk about our diets but most of us do not want to share our spending plans with anyone. The result of all of this secrecy is that we don't get support along the way. If you are uncomfortable talking about your finances with your friends, just share your Vision and not the financial part. Encouragement and accountability from family and friends will move you toward your dream much more quickly.

Prosperity Tip: We all know negative people who seem to sabotage our dreams. Share your dreams *only* with those people who will actually support you in accomplishing them.

---

5. How can I turbo-charge saving for my dream?

Have you ever noticed that the lawns that have automatic sprinkler systems are the most green and lush? This is because on a regular, systematic basis they are given water to help them flourish. Similarly, a great way to save is to create an automatic sprinkler system for your financial plan. Setting up an automatic investment plan where money is taken from your paycheck or checking account on a regular basis and sent to a savings or investment account keeps your financial garden in shape and maintained. If the timing for your Vision is near-term, consider an automatic transfer to a savings or money market account. This way the money will be available for you when you need it. If your Vision has a long-term horizon, then regularly putting your savings in a place with more growth potential might make sense for you. Consider using your retirement plan at work or setting up a systematic savings plan with an investment company for longer-term goals. Set yourself up to win—watering your financial garden will help it be lush and green.

6. What does compound interest really mean and why should I care?

Did you know that Albert Einstein described compound interest as "The greatest mathematical discovery of all time?" The magic of compound interest is simply a combination of time and rate of return on your money that grows your assets effortlessly. Here is an example. If $100 per month is invested for 30 years earning a return of 6 percent annually, that original $36,000 investment would be added to incrementally and grow to $100,452 in 30 years. That's an increase in assets of $64,452 as the result of compound interest.

7. How often do I need to check in on my goals or meet with my advisor?

It is important to keep your goals in front of you on a regular basis. If you are working on a long-term plan, make sure to check in on your financial progress at least annually but it can be as often as quarterly or monthly. If you are working with a financial advisor remember, no matter how much they care, these are still *your* goals and it is your financial future at stake! Set up reminders in your calendar to check in with your professional advisors; don't rely solely on them to do it for you. This financial review is also a great time to do a personal check-in to see if your Vision has changed or shifted. Are there new dreams you want to include in your plan? Life changes and so do our dreams. Proactively take charge of your prosperity plan.

Prosperity Steps for Action

We all know someone (maybe very intimately) who tells us that they want to lose weight and get in shape. They read the magazine articles, buy the books on the latest diet craze, and may even "try" one for a few weeks. They spend money on gym memberships and exercise

DVDs but don't seem to stick to a regimen consistently. They have an idea, even a plan, but don't seem willing to do what it really takes to improve their health. Then the cycle of guilt starts to shadow them.

The same pattern can afflict us with our Vision. Once you create a vision, the next step requires you to hold that dream in place—with your willingness to go forward and commitment to bring the dream into creation through your action plan. This is the time to show up. We keep our dreams alive with our willingness to keep our attention and commitment on the dream, the joy it gives us, our sincere desire to achieve it, and our actions. Your task is to hold your vision in place and move along the Path of Prosperity as it evolves. It absolutely will happen when you show up to support it. Some days you may fall off the path. You just have to make a contract with yourself to keep going. Realize that an action plan aligned in the pursuit of a deeply held Prosperity Vision is fun, joyful, and often effortless compared to financial plans created without your emotional investment and personal vision. You will be amazed at the speed at which your desires materialize when you are focused, willing to do what it takes, and take action.

Here are great tools to keep the spark alive and move ahead as you create your Vision. Play with them and find those that work best for you:

1. **Be willing to dive in and commit.** Ask yourself: "Am I willing to do whatever it takes to see my Vision happen?" When the answer is a resounding yes, you will see results in your life so quickly it will make your head spin! Often we don't really end up doing "whatever it takes;" the important part is to be willing to. Total conviction about your dream will bring all of the pieces together to make it a reality.

2. **Do a reality check.** Sometimes we perceive our financial situation other than it really is. A financial check-in, perhaps with advice from others, at the beginning of your action plan creation will realistically reflect where you truly are and where your financial efforts most need to be directed. Some of us overestimate how dire our situation is, while others never even want to look at their

finances: the ostrich syndrome. An early check-in with an advisor can save you lots of misplaced time and effort traveling in the wrong direction.

A 62-year-old banker named Justin told us he was terribly afraid that he would never be able to afford to retire. For months he woke up in the middle of the night worrying that he would end up living a terrible lifestyle as he grew old, and yet was afraid to take a real look at his situation. Finally, he decided to set up an appointment and check in on his financial reality. After he completed a review of his assets and savings programs as part of his Action Steps, it turned out he was already *ahead* of his target. Without a clear, in-depth look he would have continued to sit in fear of finding out he was off target.

3. **Get support along the way.** Where do you want to act alone and where do you need help? Get honest and answer whether you are a complete do-it-yourself person, a delegator, or someone in between. The financial portion of our dreams can often provoke emotions of guilt or fear or anger with internal voices such as, "I should know how to handle these issues." Decide which steps you want to execute alone or with guidance.

4. **Check your benchmarks on the Path of Prosperity.** A good action plan points the way and gives you benchmarks to measure against. That's how you track your progress, find where you need to tend to business, and know when to congratulate yourself for part of a dream achieved. Without benchmarks you can go adrift and become overwhelmed while creating your dream. For example, if you have a vision to take your children to Hawaii for a dream vacation when they are teenagers—say in five years—and you estimate the cost will be $10,000, an action plan would tell you that you need to save $4,000 towards that goal by the end of year two. Calendar and check your benchmarks regularly.

> **Prosperity Tip:** Remember: not all dreams create immediately. Often you need to take actions that lead you down the Path of Prosperity (POP). Reaching a vision is often a journey, so learn to recognize the small gifts as they occur on the path; they are opportunities to practice gratitude.

5. **Switch your attention off what isn't working and onto inspiration:** Call a "time-out" and connect with others to intentionally regain your spark. Connect with friends you admire and whom you believe are successful in life. Tell them you appreciate them and ask what techniques they use to stay on a successful track. You can also read biographies, play music, go dancing, or watch a movie to keep your enthusiasm going. These are all methods to switch your focus. Recite a daily affirmative message that inspires you to have faith and keep on the path. An attorney friend listened to the theme from the movie *Chariots of Fire* to inspire him to keep going during tough times when he was in a trial and felt his "spark" dwindling.

6. **Declutter:** Start a decluttering process immediately. Get rid of whatever clothes, papers, furniture, and books you have hanging around that you no longer need. Donate to others who can use them. Lighten your load and watch what new things come into your life. A similar method, from feng shui principles, suggests that you move 21 things in your house or office. Clean up your stuff and watch how quickly the rest of your life will change.

7. **Ramp up your giving:** Increase the energy you share with others to get back into the river of life and reconnect to your vision and actions. Engage in outflow: get up and out literally. Act *as if* you were in the flow even when you don't feel like it initially. Volunteer your time to a friend who is moving. Offer to baby-sit for someone who needs a few hours away from her kids. Volunteer a few hours to your favorite charity or religious group. Lend your

expertise to someone who could benefit from it. Get the focus off yourself and back into the network of the world.

We know a man, Frank, who was working in public accounting and became unhappy with the work. His search for the next position took longer than he expected. So instead of wallowing in his career misery, Frank decided to use this time to give back. He picked up the phone and called an organization that supported elderly people in Chicago. He soon became a "friendly" visitor to a man named Jonathan who was homebound. The weekly visits with Jonathan were wonderful for them both. And within a few weeks our friend Frank was in a new job.

8. **Last resort: if you insist, wallow in your self-pity:** Okay, last resort, go ahead and feel sorry for yourself. Don't resist...Feel it! Get into your moans and unhappiness. You might even exaggerate it to have a little fun. Brag about how bad it really is. But as you do that, whenever it feels too unhappy, remember that you have the ability to withdraw your attention from your discouragement and the beliefs that sustain it.

   You are absolutely on your way to becoming great with money if you have walked this far along the Prosperity Circle. You have important work to do and we need all of you. So please, don't overstay your time in wallow-land.

9. **Put your focus on what makes you feel good.** Just practice this next time you find yourself heading into a slump. Use our favorite shift technique by giving yourself a daily inspirational thought such as "Prosperity graces my life daily and I am grateful for it." And don't forget your Cancel! Clear! or Change the Channel tools to buoy your spirits when your thoughts take you astray.

10. **Recognize and put a name on your self-doubt:** It's really that simple. We often are chased around and around in our minds until we call the critter out...call it what it is...see it for what it is. Take all those unhelpful ideas that are starting to sabotage you on your path and name them for what they are. Say: "DOUBT" when those thoughts arise and watch them disappear or shrivel. They do not like to be identified, we promise you.

11. **Keep focused on what you want to attract, not what you don't want to attract.** There is a saying among stock traders, "There's always another train." It means that if you lose an opportunity, another is always arriving. There is much merit to that attitude. It is a simple philosophy that keeps your focus off the negative and on what you want to create, with the expectation that it will arrive and that no opportunity is really lost. People who are great with money cultivate this attitude of faith and expectation to keep their commitment. What you focus on most tends to come into your life, be it what you desire or what you fear. So focus on what you desire.

12. **Revisit your values:** Look back at your vision and drop into your feelings surrounding it and the reason you value that vision. Investigate inspirational books, websites, and movies that remind you of your vision, and the values that support it. It is a great way to refuel your commitment.

Moving from being someone who just *wishes* for prosperity in your life to someone who experiences *results* is directly related to the actions that you are willing to take. Sometimes the steps needed are large and sometimes they are small, but taking action will turn your dreams into reality.

CHAPTER 7

Turn Scarcity into Abundance

Clear Your Clutter
Unleashing the Flow
Focus Your Beliefs
Create Your Dream
Create Your
Prosperity Vision
Clarify Your Desires
Step into Action
Boldly Turn Your Vision
into Reality
Celebrate Your
Achievements
Recognize and
Receive
Express Your Gratitude
Appreciation and
Giving Back
GIVING
RECEIVING

NO MATTER WHERE YOU ARE on the Prosperity Circle, there may be moments (or sometimes days or months) when you feel financially scared, uncomfortable, or overwhelmed. Everyone has felt the worry or anxiety of financial scarcity—that trapped feeling when you are paralyzed with fear. You seem frozen, as if no action you take regarding your finances will make a difference. You are not alone in that feeling.

When it comes to money, people tend to view the world from two fundamental viewpoints: abundance or scarcity. Yet a third perspective, less familiar, is contentment: to actually enjoy where you are right now. Contentment does not necessarily relate to financial wealth. The feeling of contentment experienced by one friend meant that after graduation from college, even though his financial resources were slim, he felt content and happy where he was with his money situation. People who are great with money reside in Contentment and Abundance most often. Right now just find out which direction you flow towards. Remember to monitor your money mind-set by answering these questions:

Are you someone who believes the world never provides you enough? That making money is hard and opportunities are few? Do you feel you never attain your goals? If so, you head toward scarcity.

Or are you someone who believes that money will always flow your way and feel it always has? Or that there are limitless possibilities for you? You lean into abundance.

These are extremes and your experiences with money have likely hit both ends. Contentment and Abundance is where you will learn to live when you become great with money.

Prosperity Trap: Living with a scarcity mind-set and not being conscious of it means you believe your past experiences dictate your future. This mind-set can seriously undermine or curtail your dreams and set you up for unnecessary fears.

What a shame that so many people worry so much about money. Imagine what the world would be like if everyone came from a place of abundance and contentment.

Get Smart About Your Money Matters

One reason that financial fear and worry grip you relates to a lack of financial education. Knowledge is power when it comes to managing your financial feelings.

Prosperity Tip: You don't have to become an investment expert, but you do need to take an honest look at your finances first and then seek information to clarify any concerns. Learning helps to increase your financial confidence.

After you master the Great with Money basics in this book, especially using the strategies you have learned in the Vision and Action chapters, you will know the exact questions you want answered. That's the time to consult websites or books that provide financial specifics or tools. An example is an online financial calculator. Also, you can meet with a respected financial advisor to get an overview and become further educated. Many fears are unfounded and can be resolved by doing some research and exploring advice from a professional. At a minimum, as you work through this book, write down the questions you want to have answered as a guide for your exploration.

Switch Off Instigators of Financial Fear

The financial news media inundates us with frequent fearful messages, as well as helpful ones. Volatile markets sell papers and advertising. It is easy to get glued to the TV waiting to hear about the next big crash. When ominous messages and strong personal beliefs intersect and combine, many people finally feel compelled to act, out of feelings of scarcity and worry. But fear-based decisions are usually poor ones (this is what causes people to sell low and buy high). People are rarely rational when it comes to their money if they are stuck in a fear mind-set about their financial future. Instead, take a breath and gain perspective. When you understand your money mind-set you will make smart decisions—ones based upon your *own* vision—not one created by the media.

Prosperity Tip: Regain perspective by turning off the television periodically to calm the financial "noise."

Prosperity Steps for Controlling Financial Fear

Let's explore some tools to lift you from a scarcity mind-set into abundance.

1. Where is your attention? On scarcity or abundance?

First, practice awareness of where you are on the continuum of financial emotions containing fear, scarcity, or abundance. Check your thoughts and determine where your attention lies. For a quick quiz to assess where you are on the abundance-o-meter go to www.begreat withmoney.com.

2. Make a choice to get rid of the negatives of Bag Lady or Bogeyman.

At first it may be hard to admit that financial anxiety is a choice. We choose to visit it. Our beliefs and old experiences activate and before we know it, we are surrounded by fear and anxiety about financial matters. Then our attention becomes stuck in scarcity or fear. When this happens, stop, take a breath, and name those fears. What are they really about? Bring them out of the closet and give your fears an identity. The image that chases many women is the fear of becoming a Bag Lady. Maybe it's just the good old Bogeyman cleverly disguised as your financial worries. Whatever you see, call it out; give it a name to make your fear visible. This is a powerful and simple technique of naming and identifying to detach from your anxiety and story. If you really examine the facts, you might discover that you created a financial story in your mind, fueled it with your own negative thoughts, and started to believe it. That's how fear works. Just identifying your fear and bringing it into the open will give you some relief.

Two stories from our experiences over the years illustrate this phenomenon.

Carol, a 72-year-old woman, was dying of cancer. Her doctors told her and her family that she had no more than eight weeks to live. Carol decided that she wanted to spend the last days of her life at home and would need 24-hour care. Although it would be costly, she had enough money in her savings account to cover more than three months of care and this accounted for less than a tenth of her overall net worth. Her son (without knowing the details of his mother's financial situation) shared that she was terrified that she would run out of money if she hired 24-hour care. The fact was she could live for four years with 24-hour care and still have money left! Even on her deathbed, she could not let go of her fear of being broke.

Similarly, Leda, a 66-year-old widow, though well provided for financially by her husband upon his death, would never allow herself to fully enjoy that wealth. She remained fearful she would run out of money and held on to excessively frugal habits that were no longer warranted, given a worth in excess of $5 million. With the exception of a new home she bought, her habits tied her to Depression-era beliefs and likely thwarted much of the comfort and security her husband had worked hard to provide her upon his death.

3. Have the courage to give up your Same Old Story (SOS).

We have all had events we did not prefer: a divorce, financial loss in a business or the market, health trauma. They were real, and often the lesson gave us a nasty jolt along the path of life. The mistake, however, is to keep the past alive, especially the negative events, by retelling our story. Use the method of Same Old Story (SOS) mentioned in the Beliefs and Focus chapter. Get a grip and break your routine when you launch into your old story. Catch yourself and stop, immediately saying, "That's an old story that doesn't relate to my present life," Or "Past is smashed!" You will leave behind a past that brought you pain and unhappiness when you leave behind its story. This is a very empowering act of self-affirmation. Affirm the new person you want to create. Don't keep alive your Same Old Story. It's *past* unless you want to bring it into the present!

4. Use your toolbox.

One of the best action steps in moving up on the abundance-o-meter is to pay attention to what you say to yourself and others. Do your beliefs sound like this?

"I'll never be able to put away enough money."

"I could never have that ____."

"No one ever taught me about money so I don't understand how to make it work for me."

"I'm just not good when it comes to money."

If this sounds like your inner voice, catch it in action and use a Cancel! Clear! or Change the Channel technique on these ideas. Turn around these negative beliefs and focus your attention on an empowering belief that supports your vision. It can be as simple as "Money now flows easily and effortlessly to me."

5. Practice expecting lavish abundance.

If you feel really stuck in a story, a sure method is to create a new perspective with an "umbrella" belief, one of Lavish Abundance coming into your life. Direct your focus and help to create a new money mind-set by deliberately saying daily a phrase like "I expect, receive, and am grateful for the daily abundance that always flows in many ways into my life." This simple act can teach you to shift into an expectation of abundance. With this belief, this feeling, this vision, you will begin to see abundance appear daily.

If the words "lavish abundance" don't do it for you then find words that fit better. You can try on: Unlimited Wealth, Boundless Riches, Infinite Prosperity, Limitless Fortune, or Gobs and Gobs of Cash-a-Dough! How about "Great with Money!"

6. Turn your attention towards gratitude.

Teach yourself to review each morning or evening the actual things, events, and people you are grateful for in your life—right now. This practice will ground you in the present and bring you a sense of true fulfillment and gratitude. And it will take your attention off future or past events where fears and fantasies can build.

Remember these Prosperity Steps whenever you start to feel any financial fear. They will help to get you back on the Prosperity Circle and moving toward your dreams.

CHAPTER 8

Celebrate Your Achievements

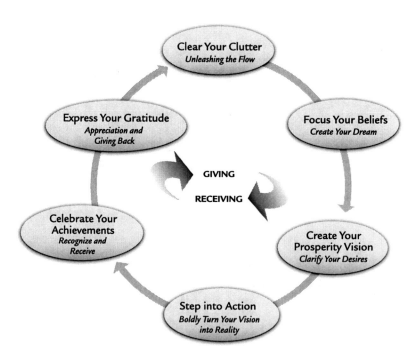

THE CELEBRATION OF ACHIEVEMENTS step in the Prosperity Circle is where the magic appears. This is the moment you see tangible results of the efforts of the previous stages. These results may come very quickly, almost instantaneously after you establish your vision, or it may take some time before your dreams **manifest.**

During this phase in the process there are three key factors to keep in mind:

1. **Pay attention** and **Recognize** that your dream has begun to appear in whole or part.

2. Take time to **celebrate** your successes as they appear.

3. Be flexible and **Make Adjustments to Navigate** your Path of Prosperity (POP) and, if needed, **Renew Commitment** to your vision.

Recognize and Receive the Gifts Along Your Path

Surprisingly, with all the effort some people put into their dream, they can miss the moment (or moments) it actually starts to manifest. How is that possible? It's a matter of where your attention is focused. If, for example, you believe your dream will only happen in the future, you fail to see the opportunities, large and small, that show up daily to support your dream and signify your progress on the path. Opportunities and blessings are everywhere when you are clearly focused on your dream; part of the fun is learning to notice and celebrate when they actually show up.

Prosperity Tip: Use a small notebook to record your "wins"—the various circumstances which occur and, bit by bit, move you closer to your realized dream.

It's easy to miss the manifestation of your vision when it appears in a form different than what you expected. Diane had a vision to do more public speaking and had set goals to get additional speaking engagements. In her mind's eye she vividly envisioned booking more opportunities to speak before a variety of groups. When she received an offer to work for a business consulting firm, she was initially concerned about how that job might conflict with her dream to speak. But then a friend pointed out that, in fact, her dream of speaking had manifested because she could design her new role as an ambassador for the consulting firm, representing them by speaking before new business groups. Voilà! The dream had manifested after all. She just needed to **recognize** it. Just as was true for Dorothy in *The Wizard of Oz*, often what we desire most is right in front of us—we just have to pay better attention.

Be flexible about the pictures that will be delivered. Stay open-minded as to how they will appear and be alert to all opportunities as they present themselves. Look for the path that opens up. Often your dream arrives in its own fashion, not in the exact way you imagined it. Also, remember to stay in an attitude of expectation. Expect your dream to be happening right now. This mental attitude helps empower your vision and keeps it continuous, so that all of the forces at work can align and present appropriate opportunities to you.

Think about the story of the man in the flood:

A Southern Illinois farmer is stuck in his home during a flood. The river is overflowing, with water rising up to his front porch. As he is standing there, a boat floats up to his house and the man in the boat says "Jump in, I'll take you to safety."

The farmer crosses his arms and says sincerely, "No, thank you, I put my trust in God. He will grant me a miracle."

The boat floats away. The water continues to rise to the second floor of his home. Another boat comes up and the man says to the farmer, who is now in the second story window, "Come in my boat, I'll save you."

The farmer says with very strong conviction, "No, thank you, I put my trust in God. He will grant me a miracle."

The boat goes away. Now the water is up to his rooftop. As the farmer stands on the roof, a helicopter comes over, and drops a ladder. The pilot yells down to the farmer, "I'll save you, climb the ladder."

The farmer mumbles with water in his mouth, "No, thank you, I put my trust in God. He will grant me a miracle."

The helicopter flies away. The floodwaters continue to rise and sweep the farmer off the roof. He drowns.

The farmer goes to heaven. God sees him and says, "What are you doing here?"

The farmer says, "I put my trust in you and you let me down. What happened to my miracle?"

God says, "What do you mean, let you down? I sent you two boats and a helicopter!!!"

Time to Celebrate and Keep Inspired

Seeing your dreams come to fruition is thrilling and fun. As you experience the results of your vision make sure to take time to celebrate your success. Sometimes the joy and surprise of a dream's manifesting creates a celebration in and of itself. Imagine how good it would feel to picture a legal parking space waiting for you just as you arrive at your destination and have it actually waiting there for you when you get there! As you pull into your parking spot, remember to smile and to thank your "parking angels" for helping you out.

When you accomplish a dream in which you have invested a great deal of energy it may feel like reaching the summit of a major mountain at last, one you have been climbing for years. The sense of pride and exhilaration is awesome. That's what the celebration felt like for Monica, mentioned in the Vision chapter, after years went by and her original vision expanded into a desire to become a lawyer. Changing her vision challenged her to go three more years to complete law school and then take and pass the bar exam...having her long-envisioned journey finally completed brought a time to truly celebrate!

Other times the win might be just a step along the way toward a bigger goal. However big or small your success is, celebrate your efforts. Share your joy with others and acknowledge their support along the way. Remember, you become an inspiration and model to others when you attain your dreams. So don't keep your success under wraps. Go ahead and be a big Great with Money person who shows others how it can be done. Stop to feel the success of your own commitment to a dream—it will inspire you and others to do more.

Be creative in finding diverse ways to celebrate your success.

Here are some ideas to consider:

- Call a friend whom you love to spend time with and celebrate together.
- Send letters of congratulations to people who have supported you along the way.
- Schedule time to experience something that you enjoy yet typically do not do such as: a trip to a museum, a walk in the park, playing with your kids, taking a long, hot bubble bath, reading a celebrity style magazine, or going to the movies in the middle of the day.
- Indulge yourself a little—remember, great with money celebrations do not need to cost great amounts of money. Get a manicure, treat your best friend to a luxuriously long lunch, eat a piece of gourmet chocolate…you get the idea!
- Give to others. Share the wealth—and express your gratitude by helping others in need.
- Party!

Be a Navigator for Your Vision and Keep Your Intention Going

We recommend using your action plan not just to get into motion but also to provide you with benchmarks to track your progress. An occasional review and monitoring of your Path of Progress along the action plan allows you to recognize when you have attained the various goals you have set for yourself. Acknowledge and celebrate each milestone achieved along the way, especially if your dream is a big one extending over time!

Remember that people who are great with money are also great navigators, constantly checking and adjusting course towards a destination. If you check your benchmarks and find that your action plan is not working quite as anticipated, remember your role as navigator. Gather information, whether it is actual data on how a particular savings plan is progressing or a harder-to-quantify progress such as cultivating networking contacts to bring you closer to your end goal.

Prosperity Tip: Actively take charge and navigate.
Take responsibility for your dream and consult with
others to decide if a shift in your action steps is necessary.
This is the value of reviewing an action plan at least
twice a year. Better yet is a check-in every three months
to make sure that you are on course. When you do
this kind of tracking you get to see how far you have come
towards your destination. If you have reached your goal,
pause to congratulate yourself on your efforts
and share the joy and success with others.

After checking your benchmarks, if you find your dream growing dimmer for you and not brighter, you need to review your beliefs and examine where your attention is focused once again. Are your thoughts aligned with your dream or is there an inner voice of doubt talking to you? Are you focused on listening to internal negativity? If so, go back and look at your dream and the declaration you wrote about it. Does it need some adjustment? You can either restate your declaration or create a new one based on changes which have evolved or in the event you have achieved your original vision. Alternatively, practice Cancel! Clear! and Change the Channel when your attention flows back to old voices that impede your dream. Review the Beliefs and Focus chapter, too, to help you realign with your dream. Often what we most desire is right around the corner; we just can't see it yet and that is when the Bogeyman of Doubt jumps out to scare us out of our dream. Use your Great with Money tools—they will carry you through the challenging moments.

Supportive friends can be a terrific help in encouraging you to keep your dreams alive and to help celebrate your achievements. Create a Great with Money Dream Team, your own Prosperity Circle of support, with like-minded positive people. Meeting on a regular basis to share your visions, checking in on action steps, and helping to keep each other accountable will add gas to the fuel tank and speed up your progress. Seek others, not to commiserate with, but to get encouragement.

If you are feeling discouraged, find people you admire and let them know of your admiration. Then ask what tools they use to carry them through any setbacks to reach success or what inspires them. Take time out to get a different perspective. Then return to your own commitment with any fresh ideas you have gained.

Expand Your World by Creating New and Exciting Visions

There is nothing quite like the feeling of having a dream come to fruition. But one thing we have learned is that it spawns a desire to put more dreams into play. If you have reached a final destination at this point, realize that manifestation of visions is an ongoing process. You will have opportunity to do this again and again throughout your life. The process just gets easier. Often the dreams begin to expand well beyond your own world into visions that impact others more significantly. So, after a hearty celebration, reflect and ask yourself, "Do I now have another vision to put in place?"

Prosperity Steps for Achievements and Celebration

To ensure you successfully reach the Celebration of Achievements stage, we invite you to use the following action steps.

1. Be accountable and deal with reality *now*, not later, later, later. Schedule a review of your progress quarterly. Sit with your advisor or another good Great with Money friend to check in and make sure you are still on track. They may see something you do not, whether it's a success to celebrate or a need for an adjustment. Remember: people who are Great with Money resemble swans more than ostriches.

2. Create a Great with Money dream team, your own Prosperity Circle of supportive people. Pick individuals from your community of friends and business acquaintances who can be supportive of your dream. Share the basic dream you are concentrating on. You need to declare to the universe what you intend to do. Then jump! Use your team as a cheering squad, reality check-in, partners along the way, or party friends. We move the world when we disclose our dreams and show our commitment. Great with Money people

inspire themselves and others when they chart and manifest their dreams. Check www.begreatwithmoney.com on a regular basis for tools and guides for creating your Prosperity Circle of support.

3. Keep a prosperity journal—write down all of your prosperity wins that move you in the direction of your dream, no matter how small. If you find a nickel on the street and add it to your savings, write it down and be grateful for money flowing to you!

4. Share your success with people who will be genuinely happy for you. If you work with financial advisors, let them know when you get a win—it will not only help you in celebrating but also help to acknowledge the advice that they are providing.

5. Enjoy the journey. Remember that the process to accomplish your dreams can be as joyous as the actual dream.

CHAPTER 9

Boost Your Prosperity with Gratitude and Appreciation

Clear Your Clutter
Unleashing the Flow

Focus Your Beliefs
Create Your Dream

Express Your Gratitude
Appreciation and Giving Back

GIVING

RECEIVING

Create Your Prosperity Vision
Clarify Your Desires

Celebrate Your Achievements
Recognize and Receive

Step into Action
Boldly Turn Your Vision into Reality

YOU HAVE NOW REACHED the final stage in the Prosperity Circle: expressing Gratitude and Appreciation. This step is not only easy to implement but also has a huge impact on your ability to be great with money—it is *the* secret to keeping your abundance flowing. Along with the cycle of Giving and Receiving, expressing your gratitude and appreciation every single day will significantly boost your progress along your Prosperity Path.

One definition of appreciation is "to recognize and be thankful for." Another definition is "an increase or rise in value, especially over time." Gratitude is defined as a "feeling of thankful appreciation for favors or benefits received." The definitions of appreciation and gratitude link together and encourage you to perform two key actions:

1. Be thankful, which leads to further growth and prosperity, and

2. Express your gratitude as the way to give back for what you receive (or envision receiving).

An outpouring of gratitude and appreciation is essential to keep prosperity flowing back to you. We have noticed an interesting phenomenon over the years. People who are most secure in their financial plans, the ones who have the greatest financial flexibility, all focus on what they are grateful for and appreciate what they have in their lives. They may share comments such as: "I have everything that I need." "We do all that we want." "It might be nice to take a bigger vacation, but if we don't, that's fine too." They focus on what they have, not what they don't have or do, and are content with it.

In contrast, people who overspend and are off track with their financial plans will talk about what they don't do or don't have. For example, we'll hear comments such as "I don't drive a big fancy car." "We don't have an updated kitchen." "We don't go out to eat that much." It's possible to tell, within a short amount of time, whether someone will reach their financial goals by merely talking to them about their lifestyle and what they desire—not even knowing about their assets.

Prosperity Tip: By expressing your thankfulness for what you *do* have, you keep your attention on growing the benefits you now enjoy. Genuine appreciation of the good in your current situation leads to actual appreciation of your financial success.

Keep Abundance Flowing

Each and every day mentally survey all that you have to be grateful for. Stop and actually recognize what you have received. End or start your day doing this or do it throughout the day. A silent moment spent in review and appreciation of all the gifts that have come to you keeps you aware of the power outside yourself that is always gifting you in diverse ways. People who are great with money find that this simple ritual helps ensure abundance. All it takes is a moment to notice, enjoy, and then express thankfulness. Daily gratitude and appreciation also inspire you to reciprocate by contributing to others, which keeps the prosperity cycle flowing.

Each night before they go to sleep Mia's children share with her five things they are grateful for. They often include things such as: "I am grateful we are a family, I am grateful for my friends, I am grateful for Ruby (the dog), etc." One night her 11-year-old son, Scott, said "I am grateful that Mommy and Daddy are so magnanimous, I am grateful that we live in such a utopia, I am grateful our lives are so fortuitous." As it turns out these were the fifth-grade spelling words that week! This gratitude ritual enables these children to focus each day on the wonderful things they have in their lives as opposed to what isn't working.

Similarly, Steven uses a daily gratitude practice of mentally expressing thanks for all the gifts of the day before he retires for sleep. He finds that this calms his mind and leads to a peaceful night's sleep.

Annie keeps a gratefulness stone she brought back from Greece. She puts it into her purse or on her desk. Then whenever she "rediscovers" it while searching through either her purse or desk, she takes the stone in her hand, pausing to reflect silently on all she is grateful for in her life at that moment.

Another act of gratitude and appreciation is the long-observed practice of tithing. In the Bible, as well as in many other religious belief systems, tithing, the act of giving some abundance back to the Divine first, was urged as an essential practice in the lives of grateful and devout people. You may have also heard of the Rule of Ten, a more contemporary expression of the tithe, which states that ten percent of your abundance should go to the source of inspiration, divine or otherwise, that provides for your abundance. These are all evidence of a universal idea that encourages the habit of appreciation and gratitude. By establishing an automatic giving account (where you have money deposited into an account monthly to be donated later) you can systematically support your giving on a regular basis.

Be a Model of Change and Inspiration for Others

Your expression of gratitude can take the form of money, words, time volunteered to another, a gift of your talent or expertise, or an in-kind donation of used items or assets. The possibilities are endless once you start to creatively and lavishly think about how to gift to others. Each of these acts is not only a way to exhibit your thankfulness but also an opportunity to make a difference for others, which will create a ripple effect in the world.

It is particularly meaningful when your demonstration of gratitude creates abundance for others. Susie is one of the most benevolent and grateful women that we know. She realized that "there by the grace of God" she was blessed to have a roof over her head and food on her table. She learned that there were too few services in her local area for homeless women and children. After doing research on this issue, Susie learned that many of these women and children become homeless after fleeing from domestic violence. Seeing the need, she joined forces with others, took action, and helped to found WINGS (Women in Need of Growing Stronger). This organization has grown steadily over the years and now has a 15,000-square-foot safe house and provides transitional services and programs to women and children. Susie's vision, her focus on how blessed her life is, has not only inspired others to give but has made a tremendous impact on the women and children who have been and continue to be served by WINGS.

The well-known actor Christopher Reeve used his quadriplegic condition as an opportunity to increase the focus to help deliver better medical care for that population. He bravely took his own physical condition not as a misfortune but as an opportunity to redirect his life, to gain funds for more medical research, and to inspire and benefit others with similar injuries.

Prosperity Tip: Consider showing your gratitude through a concept we call Sustainable Philanthropy. Make a donation that enables others to seek abundance for themselves and helps to extend prosperity to many over time.

For example, Heifer International allows donors to make gifts that assist people to build or maintain a livelihood by gifting a cow (or part of a cow), a flock of geese, or a trio of rabbits. With these gifts a family can maintain its food supply *and* create a source of income *and* provide food for others. There are also a variety of organizations providing micro-loans to people in developing countries to assist them in starting businesses. We love sustainable philanthropy as a way of showing gratitude—it is a true reflection of the Prosperity Circle. Your gift creates abundance and livelihood for others who, in turn, nurture and impact a bigger community.

Honor Your Values

When you express appreciation and gratitude through gifts and personal actions, look at the values you are endorsing in your actions. Look also at what *motivates* your giving. Are you giving to make a difference, or giving to be recognized by others? The more deliberate and connected your gifts to others, the bigger the impact you will have for your own prosperity. Are you expressing your thankfulness out of obligation or because you genuinely feel appreciative? When your expressions of gratitude are tied to your values, you feel the circle of connection to others more deeply. This connection too is part of your abundance. For example, Laura gave many hours of free legal advice to seniors, the disabled community, and people with AIDS. That pro bono service started as a way to honor her grandmother by taking care of elders. She ended up with more compassion for all these groups and their circumstances, and was graced with some deep friendships along the way.

Sometimes we show gratitude and give back just because someone asks us for support of their cause or organization. We honor their involvement and show our appreciation for the difference they are making in the world. But other times people give large contributions solely for tax benefits without much consideration of the pattern of their giving or what values they are furthering. While there is nothing inherently wrong with this, your experience of gratitude and appreciation is more fulfilling when you have thought through how and where you are spreading your wealth. People who are great with money give deliberately. Consider your giving patterns during the past year. Look at your efforts and ask, "Do my gifts match the ideals I value?" If not, boost your prosperity by putting your values back on track and in alignment with *how* you give back.

Become an Ambassador for Philanthropy

We encourage you to step up to a bigger worldview. Imagine you are a philanthropist with unlimited resources. Welcome to great with money consciousness! Where would you put your money? How would you want it to be put to work? Challenge yourself to adopt a program for giving—no matter how small—and develop a vision to increase that amount. Investigate how much you can securely gift annually or quarterly. We encourage you to make philanthropy part of your discussion, either with a financial planner or by your own planning. Do not be intimidated by your current resources for gifting! You can leverage the financial tools of life insurance or real estate to develop a plan to create and fund large charitable gifts even when your cash is limited. Share our notion of Sustainable Philanthropy with others—make gifts that both enrich others lives and provide them with the opportunity to create their own abundance.

Bring your own style to showing your thankfulness to others. Try impacting others each day with token acts of appreciation and gratitude. Have fun with your philanthropy. Send a note or e-mail to a friend (or an acquaintance) to let them know what a difference they make in your life. Pay a sincere compliment to someone you pass on the street and watch their smile. Feed someone's parking meter just so they avoid a parking ticket.

Further the idea of Pay It Forward from the movie of the same name. If someone owes you for your services or as a debt, forgo your payment. Instead, have the person "pay your debt forward" to some unknown individual and ask them to keep it going. Of course you can see that if enough of us operated by this rule of behavior, each day anyone could receive a wonderful, surprise gift which is what we believe happens already!

The real joy of philanthropy is not the recognition you might receive but your intention behind it. We do not want to diminish the idea of being acknowledged for your gift. The more important side of the equation, however, is your opportunity to express gratitude and appreciation, which then keeps the cycle of true abundance flowing for all.

Remember Your Manners

Remember what you've learned since childhood: Saying "thank you" is polite. Whether you are thanking a friend for a gift or your higher power for the blessings in your life, expressing appreciation is important. The character Eddie Haskell from the sitcom "Leave It to Beaver" thought that his politeness would get him far in life. Unfortunately, his gratitude was not sincere. As Ward Cleaver once said, "Eddie is so polite it is almost un-American." True expressions of thankfulness reward others by letting them know in a genuine manner what a difference they are making.

Prosperity Tip: Remember that giving and receiving
are *both* important. When you are being thanked,
acknowledged, or appreciated by someone else,
accept and receive those comments fully and graciously.

When you receive a "thank you" from someone, notice your response. Are you fully accepting their expression of gratitude? Reflect on how it feels if you thank someone and they respond "no problem" or "no worries." Now think how it feels if they say "you're welcome" or "it's my pleasure!"

Lisa is a mom who is particularly attuned to this concept and has taught her children to avoid saying "no problem." One day after she thanked her son Jordan for helping in the kitchen, he responded to her in his text-messaging jargon and said "N.P., Mom" (definition— no problem). Quickly catching his politeness faux pas, he said, "Oh, sorry, Mom, I mean M.P (my pleasure)!"

Matthew learned it was polite to defer a compliment so he would often say, "It's nothing," when given an appreciative remark. One day a friend challenged him on that habitual response and insisted that he actually stop and receive the appreciation of his friend. After that incident Matthew learned to really pause, take in expressions of gratitude, and to say with sincerity "Thank you. I appreciate your comments!" Remember that gratitude and appreciation are not just about the Giving part of the cycle but also about the Receiving end.

Prosperity Steps for Gratitude and Appreciation

1. Each and every day, silently or out loud, say "Thank You" for five things for which you are grateful. Continue to do this throughout the day every time you recognize a reason for gratitude. This puts your attention on receptivity. Learn to see and acknowledge the gifts you are receiving in the present moment.

2. Show your gratitude each day for one week by doing something wonderful and unexpected for someone else. Your acts can range from a verbal compliment, to a deferral of a parking space you just

acquired, to a surprise gift to a worker, to a gift of a massage for a needy friend. You decide. Be creative and be consistent for one week.

3. Select a "gratefulness stone" and put it in a purse or on a desk. When you rediscover or touch it, be prompted to recall all you are grateful for in your life at that moment.

4. Establish an automatic giving account. Determine a percentage of your net income to be set aside every month to be given to people, causes, and charities that are important and meaningful to you. You can set up a plan where money is taken systematically each month from your checking account (or directly from your pay-check) into a liquid account (savings or money market account) to be given away in the future. You will be surprised how gener-ous your giving becomes when you have an account earmarked specifically for this purpose. If your account becomes substantial in size, consult your financial advisor for more sophisticated (and possibly more tax-beneficial) ways to establish this account.

5. If you get discouraged in any way regarding your vision or prog-ress, rebalance and renew yourself by getting into an attitude of gratitude. Practice Prosperity Steps 1 or 2 above for at least three days in a row.

6. Write a check or make a donation of ten percent of your monthly salary or weekly paycheck or next commission, and send it imme-diately to any organization that has brought you true sustenance and inspiration in your life.

7. Sit down and make a list of the issues in your community or in the world you care about most. Reflect on how you might contribute *now* to the issues you value. Look into donating your time or start your own pool for annual philanthropic gifts. Start with whatever amount you have and deliberately plan how you will gift your money. Then make your gifts intentionally. Start the flow!

8. Start your own giving group or join with others who are like-minded about making a difference in the world, such as www.Kiva.org. Similar to an investment club, meet on a monthly basis to make

regular contributions to an account, research, and make contributions to causes you all desire to support.

9. Use social networking sites to build support for your cause and gather support from others. Sites such as www.DonorsChoose.org, www.Change.org, www.SixDegrees.org, www.Facebook.com, and www.MySpace.com can facilitate this.

Final Thoughts

We hope this book has helped you see that you are on your way to being truly great with money and that your joyful vision has ignited your passion and that you are truly experiencing being the designer of your life. You may have already experienced a shift in your thinking and have begun to draw in the abundance you dream of. But if you haven't, don't worry. You are on the journey of a lifetime.

The steps to a prosperous life were designed as a circle to reflect a continually flowing process. These tools will be here for you to use at any time to create whatever dreams and visions become important in your life, so we encourage you to come back to this book often. You can jump into the Prosperity Circle at any starting point to help your prosperity flow. For example, imagine things are moving along well in your financial life and then boom, all of a sudden you are faced with a potential money issue that is keeping you up at night. Let's say that you find out that the foundation of your home has a huge crack that needs to be fixed. Clearly, spending money on this repair was not part of your action plan and, indeed, may delay another goal. Instead of starting with the Clearing Clutter step, you might start by expressing your Gratitude for what is going well in your life. This will not only defuse your fear of spending the money but also allow you to focus on the blessings in your life. Next, you can check into Clearing Clutter to see if there are issues to clean up that will assist you in resolving this issue easily. Then continue on the Circle, checking in to see which tools will be most helpful.

Perhaps your vision comes to you so clearly that you want to jump right into Action to begin the process of manifesting it in your life as quickly as possible. Then, by all means, start on your action plan. If your process ever bogs down, you might review other steps such as Beliefs and Focus or Clearing Clutter to sweep your pathway clear.

If those old scarcity beliefs creep up on you, keep in mind the tools you now have to use. Remember, thoughts of lack and fear can be a huge impediment to your success. Where thought flows, energy goes.

So when a scary thought or unhelpful belief pops up, nip it in the bud! Trust that you can also use the step that speaks to you most in that moment. Often, merely activating the cycle of Giving and Receiving can restore forward motion.

We believe that as more and more of us become truly great with money, the world we will live in will be better for everyone. Please share your successes with us at www.begreatwithmoney.com—we can't wait to hear about your money magnificence!

Acknowledgments

Ellen Rogin—Acknowledgments

This book is a culmination of years of conversations about money—conversations with people in my audiences, partners, co-workers, friends, and family. There are many people who influenced this work and to whom I am deeply grateful.

To my co-author Melissa Burke, thank you for your creativity and insights. You have shown me the true impact of creative collaboration.

To Jan King, your expertise, guidance, and encouragement helped to move this book from our computers to the bookshelves. I am so glad to have met you.

Thank you to those I've had the opportunity to speak with who share their money dreams as well as their secrets. I am grateful for the work we do together. Specifically, thank you to Jeanne Splithoff. Your input on this project has been invaluable and your encouragement very much appreciated.

To Valerie Lapins, thank you so much for helping to review the book. You are not only a BFF since kindergarten, but a friend willing to give us her honest opinions. And to Tracey Kritt, girlfriend extraordinaire, thank you for listening to me talk week after week about this project during our Saturday runs. I know that it is not just because it is easier to listen than talk when you are running!

To Phyllis Campagna, you are not only the best business coach in the world (okay, for sure in my world) but also a wonderful editor, marketing consultant, and cheerleader. I so much appreciate your continual guidance and ability to see a few steps ahead of where I sometimes see myself.

I am very thankful to work with Metropolitan Capital Bank. My board service and consulting with the Private Capital Managers has helped me to grow and be inspired in many ways. Michael Rose has shown me the true power in thinking big.

To the mentors who have inspired me along the way: To Terry

Savage who has been so giving of her ideas, contacts, and experience. To Carl Guarino who helped me see that all of the parts of my life and all that I want to do can fit into one grander picture. And to Jan Black who was able to articulate in her beautiful words my vision of what is possible for me, and for the world.

I am grateful to have been a part of the Prudential Stepping Out conferences and to have worked with Mary Flowers and her team. You inspired and encouraged me to become an author and experience my own lavish abundance with respect to this project.

To the women I work with, Sandi Gore, Ann Adamson, and Susan Knight: Every day I realize how blessed I am to work with you all. Thank you for the way you all deeply care and the wonderful work that you do. I appreciate your enthusiasm about this project and the notion of taking the message out to many.

When I think about my family I realize they make everything worthwhile. My mom has always encouraged me to excel and brought me up to believe that anything is possible. To my son Benjy who has inspired me by his spiritual awareness, his connection to all beings and his belief that "there is always a way." To my daughter Amy who in her sweet, wonderful way kept me accountable to actually getting this book completed. And to my husband, Steven, who has encouraged me to live in my truth and go after all that is possible. Thank you, thank you, thank you.

Melissa Burke—Acknowledgments

Gratitude runs wide over the years for the many friends, business partners, colleagues, and family who guided and helped along my path. I am especially grateful to:

Everyone who intimately shared their life stories and dreams and provided the seeds for this book as well as lifelong service to people I truly care about;

Ellen Rogin, TBG, without whom this book would never have gone to press and with whom I love to work, play, and effortlessly learn from;

Catherine Ponder, who planted critical prosperity concepts years ago through books which continue to inspire multitudes;

Harry Palmer, founder of the Avatar® course for self-development, who created the opportunity for us to meet, provided the tools to put our book into motion, and taught how to pursue a truly great vision;

Jan King, our gracious navigator who gently knocked us up the side of our heads and kept us thoroughly on track through the pre-publication waters;

Beth Rosenthal, for mentoring, being an early reviewer, and cheering us on by keeping her book, *High Vibe Guide*, out ahead of us;

Dear friends Teresa Rupprecht, Peggy Rubenstein, Philip Steinbacher, and Jason Blake, who passed on the bounty of their talents, always left me inspired, and continue to teach me how to hold a vision in place;

Jan Black, Phyllis Campagna, Jeanne Splithoff, Valerie Lapins, and Melissa Doran for their intelligent and encouraging feedback that whipped the book into shape;

Elizabeth Winston and Janet Gutrich, busy women and generous friends who gave their time and insights for our pilot Great with Money seminar;

Manuela Soares, for taking the midnight call to advise and set us properly on the publishing road;

My family, with special loving thanks to the California contingent of Keeler, Di, Peter, Addie, Jack, Earl and Isaac, who always provided a comfort zone and place of replenishment during this writing journey.

Great with Money
Reading and Resource List

BOOKS

Assaraf, John, and Murray Smith, Murray. *The Answer: Grow Any Business, Achieve Financial Freedom, and Live an Extraordinary Life*. New York: Atria Books, 2008.

Attwood, Janet and Chris Attwood. *The Passion Test: The Effortless Path to Discovering Your Life Purpose*. New York: Penguin, 2008.

Belsky, Gary, and Thomas Gilovich. *Why Smart People Make Big Money Mistakes and How to Correct Them: Lessons from the New Science of Behavioral Economics*. New York: Simon & Schuster, 2000.

Bristol, Claude M. *The Magic of Believing*. New York: Pocket Books, 1969.

Butterworth, Eric. *Spiritual Economics: The Principles and Process of True Prosperity*. Unity Village, MO.: Unity Books (Unity School of Christianity), 2001.

Choquette, Sonia, *Your Heart's Desire: Instructions for Creating the Life You Really Want*. New York: Three Rivers Press, 1997, and more current books such as *Soul Lessons* and *Soul Purpose, Trust Your Vibes at Work* by Hay House, Inc.

Clinton, Bill. *Giving: How Each of Us Can Change the World*. New York: Alfred A. Knopf, 2007.

Edgar, Stacey. *Global Girlfriends: How One Mom Made It Her Business to Help Women in Poverty Worldwide*. New York: St Martin's Press, 2011.

Ferrazzi, Keith. *Never Eat Alone: And other Secrets to Success, One Relationship at a Time*. New York: Bantam Dell, 2005.

Gunderson, Garrett B. *Killing Sacred Cows: Overcoming Financial Myths That Are Destroying Your Prosperity*. Austin, TX: Greenleaf Book Group, 2008.

Hicks, Esther and Jerry Hicks. *Ask and It Is Given: Learning to Manifest Your Desires*. Carlsbad, CA.: Hay House, 2005.

Hill, Napoleon. *Think and Grow Rich*. New York: Tarcher, 2005.

Katie, Byron. *Loving What Is*. New York: Three Rivers Press, 2003.

Kingston, Karen. *Clear Your Clutter with Feng Shui*. New York: Broadway Books, 1999.

Needleman, Jacob. *Money and the Meaning of Life*. New York: Doubleday Publishers, 1994.

Pink, Daniel H. *A Whole New Mind: Why Right-Brainers will Rule the Future*. New York: Penguin, 2005.

Ponder, Catherine. *Dynamic Laws of Prosperity*. Camarillo, California: DeVorss & Company, 1985. Many other books by her such as *Open Your Mind to Prosperity* and *Open Your Mind to Receive*.

Post, Stephen, and Jill Neimark. *Why Good Things Happen to Good People: The Exciting New Research that Proves the Link between Doing Good and Living a Longer, Healthier, Happier Life*. New York: Broadway Books, 2007.

Robin, Vicki, and Joe Dominguez. *Your Money or Your Life: 9 Steps to Transforming Your*

Relationship with Money and Achieving Financial Independence. New York: Penguin, 2008.

Savage, Terry. *The New Savage Number: How Much Money Do You Really Need to Retire?* Hoboken, N.J.: Wiley, 2009.

Shimoff, Marci, and Carol Kline. *Happy for No Reason: 7 Steps to Being Happy from the Inside Out.* New York: Free Press, 2008.

Spangler, David. *Everyday Miracles: The Inner Art of Manifestation.* Washington: Lorian Press, 2008.

Stanny, Barbara. *Overcoming Underearning®; Overcome Your Money Fears and Earn What You Deserve,* San Francisco: Collins, 2006.

Strickland, Bill. *Make the Impossible Possible: One Man's Crusade to Inspire Others to Dream Bigger and Achieve the Extraordinary.* New York: Crown Business, 2009.

Twist, Lynne. *The Soul of Money: Reclaiming the Wealth of Our Inner Resources.* New York: W.W. Norton & Company, 2006.

Walsh, Peter. *It's All Too Much: An Easy Plan for Living a Richer Life with Less Stuff.* New York: Free Press, 2007.

RESOURCES

The Avatar Course

Avatar is a nine-day self-empowerment training involving a series of experiential exercises that enable you to rediscover your self and align your consciousness with what you want to achieve. You experience your own unique insights and revelations. It's you finding out about you. To find out more, contact Melissa@ mpburke.com or visit www.avatarepc.com and download any of their free on-line Mini-Courses. If you choose to explore further, of particular relevance is the Mini-Course on Beliefs.

Certified Financial Planner Board of Standards

www.cfpnet.org

Financial Calculators and Information

For the information, tools and support you need to earn well, save well and spend well. www.learnvest.com (Be sure to sign up for their newsletter.) To better track your spending: www.quicken.intuit.com and www.mint.com

Financial Planning Association

www.fpanet.org

Guided Mediation

Meditainment offers guided meditation, stories, natural sounds and music that help people relax and manage their thoughts. www.meditainment.com

Byron Katie

Visit Byron's site at www.thework.com and download the worksheet on the Four Questions to help you find out the difference between truth and a belief and which one controls your life.

National Association of Professional Organizers

www.napo.net

Passion Test

The Passion Test® is the simple, powerful way to discover your passions and align your life with what matters most to you, starting now. Take your personal Passion Test Profile at www.thepassiontest.com.

Psych-K™ Training

PSYCH-K is a simple and direct way to change self-limiting beliefs at the subconscious level of the mind. The practical application of this wisdom in our personal and professional lives brings a greater sense of purpose and satisfaction, mentally, emotionally, physically, and spiritually. PSYCH-K is taught world-wide by Certified PSYCH-K Instructors. **www.psych-k.com**

Volunteer Opportunities

Have you been searching for a place to volunteer close to home? VolunteerMatch strengthens communities by making it easier for good people and good causes to connect. www.volunteermatch.org

The opportunity for life-changing awareness exists in each Global Volunteers service program. Their purpose is to maintain a genuine, sustained service partnership with the host community and provide volunteers a genuine opportunity to serve. www.globalvolunteers.org

Index

About the Authors

Ellen Rogin, CPA, CERTIFIED FINANCIAL PLANNER™

A CPA, CFP® and Abundance Activist®, Ellen is a nationally known expert on living a life of success and prosperity. With more than 20 years as a business owner in the financial services industry, Ellen is a sought-after writer, speaker, and consultant, sharing her perspective that a prosperous outlook accompanied by the right financial knowledge and tools will help move you forward confidently and abundantly.

Ellen presents nationwide to corporate audiences, organizations, and associations, proposing a new and optimistic viewpoint on achieving excellence, one far greater and more meaningful than merely managing money successfully.

Ellen creates and presents marketing and training programs for her peers in the financial industry. She is also a thought-leader and trainer to coaches who desire to not only assist their clients to build prosperity but also to build their own business and personal success.

Ellen is often quoted as a financial expert in such publications as: *Money* Magazine, *Business Week, Ladies' Home Journal,* and *The Chicago Tribune.*

Ellen also serves on the board of directors for Metropolitan Capital Bank in Chicago.

Her regular practice of meditation and yoga as well as her studies of feng shui has enhanced Ellen's views of money and life. She lives in the suburbs of Chicago with her husband Steven, their children Benjy and Amy, and their very large Goldendoodle Ruby.

Please visit www.ellenrogin.com for more information on hiring Ellen to speak at your next event and for free on-line Prosperity Tips and other Great with Money resources.